Praise for *The Courage To Be Disliked*

'The ideas proffered here will certainly make you think twice about the real cause of the emotional drama in your life. A thought-provoking read.' – *Mail on Sunday*

'This thoughtful book . . . is almost spookily relevant in this age of digital one upmanship and increasing anxiety. A real game-changer.' – *Marie Claire*

'*The Courage To Be Disliked* can easily be consumed in an entire day, but its insightful, humanistic ideas will linger in the minds of readers. It's a self-help book of the most unusual variety, but by empowering people to realise that they hold all the keys to unlocking genuine happiness, it's also one of the most worthwhile things you'll read all year.' – *Culture Trip*

'...an enlightening and balanced argument that'll leave you much more aware of why you do the things you do' – *Emerald Street*

Ichiro Kishimi was born in Kyoto, where he still lives, in 1956. He has aspired to become a philosopher since his days in high school. He has researched Adlerian psychology since 1989, writing and lecturing on the subject and providing counselling for youths in psychiatric clinics as a certified counsellor and consultant for the Japanese Society of Adlerian Psychology. He is the translator, into Japanese, of selected writings by Alfred Adler, and he is the author of *Adora Shinrigaku Nyumon* (Introduction to Adlerian Psychology), in addition to numerous other books.

Fumitake Koga, an award-winning professional writer and author, was born in 1973. He has released numerous bestselling works of business-related and general non-fiction. He encountered Adlerian psychology in his late twenties and was deeply affected by its conventional wisdom-defying ideas. Thereafter, Koga made numerous visits to Ichiro Kishimi in Kyoto, gleaned from him the essence of Adlerian psychology and took down the notes for the classical 'dialogue format' method of Greek philosophy that is used in this book.

THE
COURAGE
TO BE DISLIKED

How to free yourself, change
your life and achieve real
happiness

ICHIRO KISHIMI and FUMITAKE KOGA

ALLEN&UNWIN

First published in Japan as *Kirawareru Yuki* by Diamond Inc., Tokyo, in 2013

First published in the United Kingdom by Allen & Unwin in 2018

This paperback edition published in 2019

This English-language edition published by arrangement with Diamond Inc. in care of Tuttle-Mori Agency Inc., Tokyo, through Chandler Crawford Agency, Massachusetts, USA.

Allen & Unwin
c/o Atlantic Books
Ormond House
26–27 Boswell Street
London WC1N 3JZ
Phone: 020 7269 1610
Fax: 020 7430 0916
Email: UK@allenandunwin.com
Web: www.allenandunwin.com/uk

A CIP catalogue record for this book is available from the British Library.

Paperback ISBN 978 1 76063 073 7
E-Book ISBN 978 1 76063 826 9

Printed and bound by CPI Group (UK) Ltd, Croydon, CR0 4YY

AUTHORS' NOTE

Sigmund Freud, Carl Jung and Alfred Adler are all giants in the world of psychology. This book is a distillation of Adler's philosophical and psychological ideas and teachings, taking the form of a narrative dialogue between a philosopher and a young man.

Adlerian psychology enjoys a broad base of support in Europe and the USA, and presents simple and straightforward answers to the philosophical question: how can one be happy? Adlerian psychology might hold the key. Reading this book could change your life. Now, let us accompany the young man and venture beyond the 'door'.

CONTENTS

THE THIRD NIGHT
Discard other people's tasks

THE FOURTH NIGHT
Where the centre of the world is

THE FIFTH NIGHT
To live in earnest in the here and now

On the outskirts of the thousand-
year-old city lived a philosopher who
taught that the world was simple and
that happiness was within the reach
of every man, instantly. A young
man who was dissatisfied with life
went to visit this philosopher to
get to the heart of the matter. This
youth found the world a chaotic
mass of contradictions and, in
his anxious eyes, any notion of
happiness was completely absurd.

INTRODUCTION

YOUTH: I want to ask you once again; you do believe that the world is, in all ways, a simple place?

PHILOSOPHER: Yes, this world is astonishingly simple and life itself is, too.

YOUTH: So, is this your idealistic argument or is it a workable theory? What I mean is, are you saying that any issues you or I face in life are simple too?

PHILOSOPHER: Yes, of course.

YOUTH: Alright then, but let me explain why I have come to visit you today. Firstly, I want to debate this with you until I am satisfied, and then, if possible, I want to get you to retract this theory.

PHILOSOPHER: Ha-ha.

YOUTH: Because I have heard all about your reputation. The word is that there is an eccentric philosopher living here whose teachings and arguments are hard to ignore, namely, that people can change, that the world is simple and that everyone can be happy. That is the sort of thing I have heard, but I find that view totally unacceptable, so I wanted to confirm things for myself. If I find anything you say completely off, I will point it out and then correct you . . . But will you find that annoying?

PHILOSOPHER: No, I would welcome the opportunity. I have been hoping to hear from a young person just like you and to learn as much as possible from what you can tell me.

YOUTH: Thanks. I do not intend to dismiss you out of hand. I will take your views into consideration and then look at the possibilities that present themselves. 'The world is simple and life is simple too'—if there is anything in this thesis that might contain truth, it would be life from a child's point of view. Children do not have any obvious duties, like paying taxes or going to work. They are protected by their parents and society, and can spend days free from care. They can imagine a future that goes on forever and do whatever they want. They don't have to see grim reality—they are blindfolded. So, to them the world must have a simple form. However, as a child matures to adulthood the world reveals its true nature. Very shortly, the child will know how things really are and what he is really allowed to do. His opinion will alter and all he will see is impossibility. His romantic view will end and be replaced by cruel realism.

PHILOSOPHER: I see. That is an interesting view.

YOUTH: That's not all. Once grown up, the child will get entangled in all kinds of complicated relationships with people and have all kinds of responsibilities thrust upon him. That is how life will be, both at work and at home, and in any role he assumes in public life. It goes without saying that he will become aware of the various issues in society that he couldn't understand as a child, including discrimination, war and inequality, and he will not be able to ignore them. Am I wrong?

PHILOSOPHER: It sounds fine to me. Please continue.

YOUTH: Well, if we were still living at a time when religion held sway, salvation might be an option, because the teachings of the divine were everything to us. All we had to do was obey them and consequently have little to think about. But religion has lost its power and now there is no real belief in God. With nothing to rely on, everyone is filled with anxiety and doubt. Everyone is living for themselves. That is how society is today, so please tell me—given these realities and in the light of what I have said—can you still say the world is simple?

PHILOSOPHER: There is no change in what I say. The world is simple and life is simple too.

YOUTH: How? Anyone can see that it's a chaotic mass of contradictions.

PHILOSOPHER: That is not because the world is complicated. It's because you are *making* the world complicated.

YOUTH: I am?

PHILOSOPHER: None of us live in an objective world, but instead in a subjective world that we ourselves have given meaning to. The world you see is different from the one I see, and it's impossible to share your world with anyone else.

YOUTH: How can that be? You and I are living in the same country, in the same time, and we are seeing the same things—aren't we?

PHILOSOPHER: You look rather young to me, but have you ever drunk well water that has just been drawn?

YOUTH: Well water? Um, it was a long time ago, but there was a well at my grandmother's house in the countryside. I remember enjoying the fresh, cold water drawn from that well on a hot summer's day.

PHILOSOPHER: You may know this, but well water stays at pretty much the same temperature all year round, at about 18 degrees. That is an objective number—it stays the same to everyone who measures it. But when you drink the water in the summer it seems cool and when you drink the same water in the winter it seems warm. Even though it's the same water, at the same 18 degrees according to the thermometer, the way it seems depends on whether it's summer or winter.

YOUTH: So, it's an illusion caused by the change in the environment.

PHILOSOPHER: No, it's not an illusion. You see, to you, in that moment, the coolness or warmth of the well water is an undeniable fact. That's what it means to live in your subjective world. There is no escape from your own subjectivity. At present, the world seems complicated and mysterious to you, but if you change, the world will appear more simple. The issue is not about how the world is, but about how you are.

YOUTH: How I am?

PHILOSOPHER: Right . . . It's as if you see the world through dark glasses, so naturally everything seems dark. But if that is the case, instead of lamenting about the world's darkness, you could just remove the glasses. Perhaps the world will appear terribly bright to you then and you will involuntarily shut your eyes. Maybe you'll want the glasses back on, but can you even take them off in the first place? Can you look directly at the world? Do you have the courage?

YOUTH: Courage?

PHILOSOPHER: Yes, it's a matter of courage.

YOUTH: Well alright. There are tons of objections I would like to raise, but I get the feeling it would be better to go into them later. I would like to confirm that you are saying 'people can change', right?

PHILOSOPHER: Of course people can change. They can also find happiness.

YOUTH: Everyone, without exception?

PHILOSOPHER: No exceptions whatsoever.

YOUTH: Ha-ha! Now you're talking big! This is getting interesting. I'm going to start arguing with you immediately.

PHILOSOPHER: I am not going to run away or hide anything. Let's take our time debating this. So, your position is 'people cannot change?'

YOUTH: That's right, they can't change. Actually, I am suffering myself because of not being able to change.

PHILOSOPHER: And at the same time, you wish you could.

YOUTH: Of course. If I could change, if I could start life all over again, I would gladly fall to my knees before you. But it could turn out that you'll be down on your knees before me.

PHILOSOPHER: You remind me of myself during my own student days, when I was a hot-blooded young man searching for the truth, traipsing about, calling on philosophers . . .

YOUTH: Yes. I am searching for the truth. The truth about life.

PHILOSOPHER: I have never felt the need to take in disciples and have never done so. However, since becoming a student of Greek philosophy and then coming into contact with another philosophy, I have been waiting for a long time for a visit from a young person like you.

YOUTH: Another philosophy? What would that be?

PHILOSOPHER: My study is just over there. Go into it. It's going to be a long night. I will go and make some hot coffee.

THE
FIRST
NIGHT

Deny trauma

The young man entered the study and sat slouched in a chair. Why was he so determined to reject the philosopher's theories? His reasons were abundantly clear. He lacked self-confidence and, ever since childhood, this had been compounded by deep-seated feelings of inferiority with regard to his personal and academic backgrounds, as well as his physical appearance. Perhaps, as a result, he tended to be excessively self-conscious when people looked at him. Mostly, he seemed incapable of truly appreciating other people's happiness, and was constantly pitying himself.
To him, the philosopher's claims were nothing more than the stuff of fantasy.

THE UNKNOWN 'THIRD GIANT'

YOUTH: A moment ago, you used the words 'another philosophy', but I've heard that your specialty is in Greek philosophy.

PHILOSOPHER: Yes, Greek philosophy has been central to my life ever since I was a teenager. The great intellectual figures: Socrates, Plato, Aristotle. I am translating a work by Plato at the moment, and I expect to spend the rest of my life studying classical Greek thought.

YOUTH: Well, then what is this 'other philosophy'?

PHILOSOPHER: It is a completely new school of psychology that was established by the Austrian psychiatrist, Alfred Adler, at the beginning of the twentieth century. In this country, it is generally referred to as Adlerian psychology.

YOUTH: Huh. I never would have imagined that a specialist in Greek philosophy would be interested in psychology.

PHILOSOPHER: I'm not very familiar with paths taken by other schools of psychology. However, I think it is fair to say that Adlerian psychology is clearly in line with Greek philosophy, and that it is a proper field of study.

YOUTH: I have a passing knowledge of the psychology of Freud and Jung. A fascinating field.

PHILOSOPHER: Yes, Freud and Jung are both renowned. Even here. Adler was one of the original core members of the Vienna Psychoanalytic Society, which was led by Freud. His ideas were counter to Freud's, and he split from the group and proposed an 'individual psychology' based on his own original theories.

YOUTH: Individual psychology? Another odd term. So, Adler was a disciple of Freud's?

PHILOSOPHER: No, he was not. That misconception is common; we must dispel it. For one thing, Adler and Freud were relatively close in age, and the relationship they formed as researchers was founded upon equal footing. In this respect, Adler was very different from Jung, who revered Freud as a father figure. Though psychology primarily tends to be associated with Freud and Jung, Adler is recognised throughout the rest of the world, along with Freud and Jung, as one of the three giants in this field.

YOUTH: I see. I should have studied it more.

PHILOSOPHER: I suppose it's only natural you haven't heard of Adler. As he himself said, 'There might come a time when one will not remember my name; people might even have forgotten that our school ever existed.' Then he went on to say that it didn't matter. The implication being that if his school were forgotten, it would be because his ideas had outgrown the bounds of a single area of scholarship, and become commonplace, and a feeling shared by everyone. For example, Dale Carnegie, who wrote the international bestsellers *How to Win Friends and Influence People* and *How to Stop Worrying and Start Living*, referred to Adler as 'a great psychologist who devoted his life to researching humans and their latent abilities'. The influence of Adler's thinking is clearly present throughout his writings. And in Stephen Covey's *The 7 Habits of Highly Effective People*, much of the content closely resembles Adler's ideas. In other words, rather than being a strict area of scholarship, Adlerian psychology is accepted as a realisation; a culmination of truths and of human understanding. Yet Adler's ideas are said to have been a hundred years ahead of their time, and even today we have not managed to fully comprehend them. That is how truly ground breaking they were.

YOUTH: So, your theories are developed not from Greek philosophy initially, but from the viewpoint of Adlerian psychology?

PHILOSOPHER: Yes, that's right.

YOUTH: Okay. There's one more thing I'd like to ask about your basic stance. Are you a philosopher? Or are you a psychologist?

PHILOSOPHER: I am a philosopher; a person who lives philosophy. And, for me, Adlerian psychology is a form of thought that is in line with Greek philosophy, and that *is* philosophy.

YOUTH: All right then. Let's get started.

WHY PEOPLE CAN CHANGE

YOUTH: First, let's plan the points of discussion. You say people can change. Then you take it a step farther, saying that everyone can find happiness.

PHILOSOPHER: Yes, everyone, without exception.

YOUTH: Let's save the discussion about happiness for later and address change first. Everyone wishes they could change. I know I do, and I'm sure anyone you might stop and ask on the street would agree. But why does everyone feel they want to change? There's only one answer: because they cannot change. If it were easy for people to change, they wouldn't spend so much time wishing they could. No matter how much they wish it, people cannot change. And that's why there are always so many people getting taken in by new religions and dubious self-help seminars, and any preaching on how everyone can change. Am I wrong?

PHILOSOPHER: Well, in response, I'd ask why you are so adamant that people can't change.

YOUTH: Here's why. I have a friend, a guy, who has shut himself in his room for several years. He wishes he could go out, and even thinks he'd like to have a job, if possible. So, he wants to change the way he is. I say this as his friend, but I assure you he is a very serious person who could be of great use to society. Except that he's afraid to leave his room. If he takes even a single step outside, he suffers palpitations and his arms and legs shake. It's a kind of neurosis or panic, I suppose. He wants to change, but he can't.

PHILOSOPHER: What do you think the reason is that he can't go out?

YOUTH: I'm not really sure. It could be because of his relationship with his parents, or because he was bullied at school or work. He might have experienced a kind of trauma from something like that. But then, it could be the opposite—maybe he was too pampered as a child and can't face reality. I just don't know, and I can't pry into his past or his family situation.

PHILOSOPHER: So, you are saying there were incidents in your friend's past that became the cause of trauma, or something similar, and as a result he can't go out anymore?

YOUTH: Of course. Before an effect, there's a cause. There is nothing mysterious about that.

PHILOSOPHER: Then perhaps the cause of his not being able to go out anymore lies in the home environment during his childhood. He was abused by his parents and reached adulthood without ever feeling love. That's why he's afraid of interacting with people and why he can't go out. It's feasible, isn't it?

YOUTH: Yes, it's entirely feasible. I'd imagine that would be really challenging.

PHILOSOPHER: And then you say, 'Before an effect, there's a cause.' Or, in other words, who I am now (the effect) is determined by occurrences in the past (the causes). Do I understand correctly?

YOUTH: You do.

PHILOSOPHER: So, if the here and now of everyone in the world is due to their past incidents, according to you, wouldn't things turn out very strangely? Don't you see? Everyone who has grown up abused by his or her parents would have to suffer the same effects as your friend and become a recluse, or the whole idea just doesn't hold water. That is, if the past actually determines the present, and the causes control the effects.

YOUTH: What, exactly, are you getting at?

PHILOSOPHER: If we focus only on past causes and try to explain things solely through cause and effect, we end up with 'determinism'. Because what this says is that our present and our future have already been decided by past occurrences, and are unalterable. Am I wrong?

YOUTH: So, you're saying that the past doesn't matter?

PHILOSOPHER: Yes, that is the standpoint of Adlerian psychology.

YOUTH: I see. The points of conflict seem a bit clearer. But look, if we go by your version, wouldn't that ultimately mean that there's no reason my friend can't go out anymore? Because you're saying that past incidents don't matter. I'm sorry, but that's completely out of the question. There has to be some reason behind his seclusion. There has to be, or there'd be no explanation!

PHILOSOPHER: Indeed, there would be no explanation. So, in Adlerian psychology, we do not think about past 'causes', but rather about present 'goals'.

YOUTH: Present goals?

PHILOSOPHER: Your friend is insecure, so he can't go out. Think about it the other way around. He doesn't want to go out, so he's creating a state of anxiety.

YOUTH: Huh?

PHILOSOPHER: Think about it this way. Your friend had the goal of not going out beforehand, and he's been manufacturing a state of anxiety and fear as a means to achieve that goal. In Adlerian psychology, this is called 'teleology'.

YOUTH: You're joking! My friend has imagined his anxiety and fear? So, would you go so far as saying that my friend is just pretending to be sick?

PHILOSOPHER: He is not pretending to be sick. The anxiety and fear your friend is feeling are real. On occasion, he might also suffer from migraines and violent stomach cramps. However, these too are symptoms that he has created in order to achieve the goal of not going out.

YOUTH: That's not true! No way! That's too depressing!

PHILOSOPHER: No. This is the difference between 'aetiology' (the study of causation) and teleology (the study of the purpose of a given phenomenon, rather than its cause). Everything you have been telling me is based in aetiology. As long as we stay in aetiology, we will not take a single step forward.

TRAUMA DOES NOT EXIST

YOUTH: If you are going to state things so forcibly, I'd like a thorough explanation. To begin with, what is the difference you refer to between aetiology and teleology?

PHILOSOPHER: Supposing you've got a cold with a high fever, and you've gone to see the doctor. Then, suppose the doctor says the reason for your sickness is that yesterday, when you went out, you weren't dressed well enough, and that's why you've caught a cold. Now, would you be satisfied with that?

YOUTH: Of course I wouldn't. It wouldn't matter to me what the reason was—the way I was dressed or because it was raining, or whatever. It's the symptoms, the fact that I'm suffering with a high fever now that would matter to me. If he's a doctor, I'd need him to treat me by prescribing medicine, giving shots or taking whatever specialised measures are necessary.

PHILOSOPHER: Yet those who take an aetiological stance, including most counsellors and psychiatrists, would argue that what you were suffering from stemmed from such-and-such cause in the past, and would then end up just consoling you by saying, 'So you see, it's not your fault.' The argument concerning so-called traumas is typical of aetiology.

YOUTH: Wait a minute! Are you denying the existence of trauma altogether?

PHILOSOPHER: Yes, I am. Adamantly.

YOUTH: What! Aren't you, or I guess I should say Adler, an authority on psychology?

PHILOSOPHER: In Adlerian psychology, trauma is definitively denied. This was a very new and revolutionary point. Certainly, the Freudian view of trauma is fascinating. Freud's idea is that a person's psychic wounds (traumas) cause his or her present unhappiness. When you treat a person's life as a vast narrative, there is an easily understandable causality and sense of dramatic development that creates strong impressions and is extremely attractive. But Adler, in denial of the trauma argument, states the following: 'No experience is in itself a cause of our success or failure. We do not suffer from the shock of our experiences—the so-called trauma—but instead we make out of them whatever suits our purposes. We are not determined by our experiences, but the meaning we give them is self-determining.'

YOUTH: So, we make of them whatever suits our purposes?

PHILOSOPHER: Exactly. Focus on the point Adler is making here when he refers to the self being determined not by our experiences themselves, but by *the meaning we give them.* He is not saying that the experience of a horrible calamity or abuse during childhood or other such incidents have no influence on forming a personality; their influences are strong. But the important thing is that nothing is actually determined by those influences. We determine our own lives according to the meaning we give to those past experiences. Your life is not something that someone gives you, but something you choose yourself, and you are the one who decides how you live.

YOUTH: Okay, so you're saying that my friend has shut himself in his room because he actually chooses to live this way? This is serious. Believe me, it is not what he wants. If anything, it's something he was forced to choose because of circumstances. He had no choice other than to become who he is now.

PHILOSOPHER: No. Even supposing that your friend actually thinks *I can't fit into society because I was abused by my parents*, it's still because it is his *goal* to think that way.

YOUTH: What sort of goal is that?

PHILOSOPHER: The immediate thing would probably be the goal of 'not going out'. He is creating anxiety and fear as his reasons to stay inside.

YOUTH: But why doesn't he want to go out? That's where the problem resides.

PHILOSOPHER: Well, think of it from the parents' view. How would you feel if your child were shut up in a room?

YOUTH: I'd be worried, of course. I'd want to help him return to society; I'd want him to be well, and I'd wonder if I'd raised him improperly. I'm sure I would be seriously concerned, and try in every way imaginable to help him back to a normal existence.

PHILOSOPHER: *That* is where the problem is.

YOUTH: Where?

PHILOSOPHER: If I stay in my room all the time, without ever going out, my parents will worry. I can get all of my parents' attention focused on me. They'll be extremely careful around me, and always handle me with kid gloves. On the other hand, if I take even one step out of the house, I'll just become part of a faceless mass who no one pays attention to. I'll be surrounded by people I don't know, and just end up average, or less than average. And no one will take special care of me any longer . . . Such stories about reclusive people are not uncommon.

YOUTH: In that case, following your line of reasoning, my friend has accomplished his goal, and is satisfied with his current situation?

PHILOSOPHER: I doubt he's satisfied, and I'm sure he's not happy either. But there is no doubt that he is also taking action in line with his goal. This is not something that is unique to your friend. Every one of us is living in line with some goal. That is what teleology tells us.

YOUTH: No way. I reject that as completely unacceptable. Look, my friend is—

PHILOSOPHER: Listen, this discussion won't go anywhere if we just keep talking about your friend. It will turn into a trial in absentia, and that would be hopeless. Let's use another example.

YOUTH: Well, how about this one? It's my own story about something I experienced only yesterday.

PHILOSOPHER: Oh? I'm all ears.

PEOPLE FABRICATE ANGER

YOUTH: Yesterday afternoon, I was reading a book in a coffee shop when a waiter passed by and spilled coffee on my jacket. I'd just bought it and it's my nicest piece of clothing. I couldn't help it; I just blew my top. I yelled at him at the top of my lungs. I'm not normally the type of person who speaks loudly in public places. But yesterday, the shop was ringing with the sound of my shouting because I flew into a rage and forgot what I was doing. So, how about that? Is there any room for a goal to be involved here? No matter how you look at it, isn't this behaviour that originates from a cause?

PHILOSOPHER: So, you were stimulated by the emotion of anger, and ended up shouting. Though you are normally mild-mannered, you couldn't resist being angry. It was an unavoidable occurrence, and you couldn't do anything about it. Is that what you are saying?

YOUTH: Yes, because it happened so suddenly. The words just came out of my mouth before I had time to think.

PHILOSOPHER: Then just suppose you happened to have had a knife on you yesterday, and when you blew up you just got carried away and stabbed him. Would you still be able to justify that by saying, 'It was an unavoidable occurrence, and I couldn't do anything about it'?

YOUTH: That . . . Come on, that's an extreme argument!

PHILOSOPHER: It is not an extreme argument. If we proceed with your reasoning, any offence committed in anger can be blamed on anger, and will no longer be the responsibility of the person because, essentially, you are saying that people cannot control their emotions.

YOUTH: Well, how do you explain my anger then?

PHILOSOPHER: That's easy. You did not fly into a rage and then start shouting. It is solely that you got angry so that you could shout. In other words, in order to fulfil the goal of shouting, you created the emotion of anger.

YOUTH: What do you mean?

PHILOSOPHER: The goal of shouting came before anything else. That is to say, by shouting, you wanted to make the waiter submit to you and listen to what you had to say. As a means to do that, you fabricated the emotion of anger.

YOUTH: I fabricated it? You've got to be joking!

PHILOSOPHER: Then why did you raise your voice?

YOUTH: As I said before, I blew my top. I was deeply frustrated.

PHILOSOPHER: No. You could have explained matters without raising your voice, and the waiter would most likely have given you a sincere apology, wiped your jacket with a clean cloth, and taken other appropriate measures. He might have even arranged for it to be dry-cleaned. And somewhere in your mind, you were anticipating that he might do these things but, even so, you shouted. The procedure of explaining things in normal words felt like too much trouble, and you tried to get out of that and make this unresisting person submit to you. The tool you used to do this was the emotion of anger.

YOUTH: No way. You can't fool me. I manufactured anger in order to make him submit to me? I swear to you, there wasn't even a second to think of such a thing. I didn't think it over and then get angry. Anger is a more impulsive emotion.

PHILOSOPHER: That's right, anger is an instantaneous emotion. Now listen, I have a story. One day, a mother and daughter were quarrelling loudly. Then, suddenly, the telephone rang. 'Hello?' The mother picked up the receiver hurriedly, her voice still thick with anger. The caller was her daughter's homeroom teacher. As soon as the mother realised who was phoning, the tone of her voice changed and she became very polite. Then, for the next five minutes or so, she carried on a conversation in her best telephone voice. Once she hung up, in a moment, her expression changed again and she went straight back to yelling at her daughter.

YOUTH: Well, that's not a particularly unusual story.

PHILOSOPHER: Don't you see? In a word, anger is a tool that can be taken out as needed. It can be put away the moment the phone rings, and pulled out again after one hangs up. The mother isn't yelling in anger she cannot control. She is simply using the anger to overpower her daughter with a loud voice, and thereby assert her opinions.

YOUTH: So, anger is a means to achieve a goal?

PHILOSOPHER: That is what teleology says.

YOUTH: Ah, I see now. Under that gentle-looking mask you wear, you're terribly nihilistic! Whether we're talking about anger or my reclusive friend, all your insights are stuffed with feelings of distrust for human beings!

HOW TO LIVE WITHOUT BEING CONTROLLED BY THE PAST

PHILOSOPHER: How am I being nihilistic?

YOUTH: Think about it. Simply put, you deny human emotion. You say that emotions are nothing more than tools; that they're just the means for achieving goals. But listen. If you deny emotion, you're upholding a view that tries to deny our humanity, too. Because it's our emotions, and the fact that we are swayed by all sorts of feelings that make us human. If emotions are denied, humans will be nothing more than poor excuses for machines. If that isn't nihilism, then what is?

PHILOSOPHER: I am not denying that emotion exists. Everyone has emotions. That goes without saying. But if you are going to tell me that people are beings who can't resist emotion, I'd argue against that. Adlerian psychology is a form of thought, a philosophy that is diametrically opposed to nihilism. We are not controlled by emotion. In this sense, while it shows that 'people are not controlled by emotion', additionally it shows that 'we are not controlled by the past'.

YOUTH: So, people are not controlled either by emotion or the past?

PHILOSOPHER: Okay, for example, suppose there is someone whose parents had divorced in his past. Isn't this something objective, the same as the well water that is always eighteen degrees? But then, does that divorce feel cold or does it feel warm? So, this is a 'now' thing, a subjective thing. Regardless of what may have happened in the past, it is the meaning that is attributed to it that determines the way someone's present will be.

YOUTH: The question isn't 'what happened?', but 'how was it resolved?'

PHILOSOPHER: Exactly. We can't go back to the past in a time machine. We can't turn back the hands of time. If you end up staying in aetiology, you will be bound by the past and never be able to find happiness.

YOUTH: That's right! We can't change the past, and that's precisely why life is so hard.

PHILOSOPHER: Life isn't just hard. If the past determined everything and couldn't be changed, we who are living today would no longer be able to take effective steps forward in our lives. What would happen as a result? We would end up with the kind of nihilism and pessimism that loses hope in the world and gives up on life. The Freudian aetiology that is typified by the trauma argument is determinism in a different form, and is the road to nihilism. Are you going to accept values like that?

YOUTH: I don't want to accept them, but the past is so powerful.

PHILOSOPHER: Think of the possibilities. If one assumes that people are beings who can change, a set of values based on aetiology becomes untenable, and one is compelled to take the position of teleology as a matter of course.

YOUTH: So, you are saying that one should always take the 'people can change' premise?

PHILOSOPHER: Of course. And, please understand, it is Freudian aetiology that denies our free will, and treats humans like machines.

The young man paused and glanced around the philosopher's study. Floor-to-ceiling bookshelves filled the walls, and on a small wooden desk lay a fountain pen and what appeared to be a partially written manuscript. 'People are not driven by past causes, but move toward goals that they themselves set'—that was the philosopher's claim. The teleology he espoused was an idea that overturned at the root the causality of respectable psychology, and the young man found that impossible to accept. So, from which standpoint should he start to argue it? The youth took a deep breath.

SOCRATES AND ADLER

YOUTH: All right. Let me tell you about another friend of mine, a man named Y. He's the kind of person who has always had a bright personality and talks easily to anyone. He's like a sunflower—everyone loves him, and people smile whenever he's around. In contrast, I am someone who has never had an easy time socially, and who's kind of warped in various ways. Now, you are claiming that people can change through Adler's teleology?

PHILOSOPHER: Yes. You, I and everyone can change.

YOUTH: Then, do you think I could become someone like Y? From the bottom of my heart, I really wish I could be like him.

PHILOSOPHER: At this point, I'd have to say that's totally out of the question.

YOUTH: Aha! Now you're showing your true colours! So, are you going to retract your theory?

PHILOSOPHER: No, I am not. Unfortunately, you have almost no understanding of Adlerian psychology yet. The first step to change is knowing.

YOUTH: So, if I can understand just something about Adlerian psychology, can I become a person like Y?

PHILOSOPHER: Why are you rushing for answers? You should arrive at answers on your own, and not rely upon what you get from someone else. Answers from others are nothing more than stopgap measures; they're of no value. Take Socrates, who left not one book actually written by himself. He spent his days having public debates with the citizens of Athens, especially the young, and it was his disciple, Plato, who put his philosophy into writing for future generations. Adler, too, showed little interest in literary activities, preferring to engage in personal dialogue at cafés in Vienna, and hold small discussion groups. He was definitely not an armchair intellectual.

YOUTH: So, Socrates and Adler both conveyed their ideas by dialogue?

PHILOSOPHER: That's right. All your doubts will be dispelled through this dialogue. And you will begin to change. Not by my words, but by your own doing. I do not want to take away that valuable process of arriving at answers through dialogue.

YOUTH: So, are we going to try and re-enact the kind of dialogue that Socrates and Adler carried out? In this little study?

PHILOSOPHER: Isn't that good enough for you?

YOUTH: That's what I'm hoping to find out! So, let's take it as far as we can, until either you retract your theory or I bow before you.

ARE YOU OKAY JUST AS YOU ARE?

PHILOSOPHER: Okay, let's go back to your query. So, you'd like to be a more upbeat person, like Y?

YOUTH: But you just rejected that, and said it was out of the question. Well, I guess that's just how it is. I was just saying that to give you a hard time—I know myself well enough. I could never be someone like that.

PHILOSOPHER: Why not?

YOUTH: It's obvious. Because we have different personalities, or I guess you could say dispositions.

PHILOSOPHER: Hmm.

YOUTH: You, for instance, live surrounded by all these books. You read a new book and gain new knowledge. Basically, you keep accumulating knowledge. The more you read, the more your knowledge increases. You find new concepts of value, and it seems to you that they change you. Look, I hate to break it to you, but no matter how much knowledge you gain, your disposition or personality isn't going to basically change. If your base gets skewed, all you've learned will be useless. Yes, all the knowledge you've acquired will come crashing down around you, and then the next thing you know, you'll be back to where you started! And the same goes for Adler's ideas. No matter how many facts I may try to accumulate about him, they're not going to have any effect on my personality. Knowledge just gets piled up as knowledge, until sooner or later it's discarded.

PHILOSOPHER: Then let me ask you this. Why do you think you want to be like Y? I guess you just want to be a different person, whether it's Y or someone else. But what is the goal of that?

YOUTH: You're talking about goals again? As I said earlier, it's just that I admire him and I think I'd be happier if I were like him.

PHILOSOPHER: You think you'd be happier if you were like him. Which means that you are not happy now, right?

YOUTH: What!

PHILOSOPHER: Right now, you are unable to feel really happy. This is because you have not learned to love yourself. And to try to love yourself, you are wishing to be reborn as a different person. You're hoping to become like Y, and throw away who you are now. Correct?

YOUTH: Yes, I guess that's right! Let's face it: I hate myself! I, the one who's doing this playing around with old-fashioned philosophical discourse, and who just can't help doing this sort of thing—yes, I really hate myself.

PHILOSOPHER: That's all right. If you were to ask around for people who say they like themselves, you'd be hard pressed to find someone who'd puff up their chest with pride and say, 'Yes, I like myself.'

YOUTH: How about you? Do you like yourself?

PHILOSOPHER: At the very least, I do not think I would like to be a different person and I accept who I am.

YOUTH: You accept who you are?

PHILOSOPHER: Look, no matter how much you want to be Y, you cannot be reborn as him. You are not Y. It's okay for you to be you. However, I am not saying it's fine to be 'just as you are'. If you are unable to really feel happy, then it's clear that things aren't right just as they are. You've got to put one foot in front of the other, and not stop.

YOUTH: That's a harsh way of putting it, but I get your point. It's clear that I'm not right just the way I am. I've got to move forward.

PHILOSOPHER: To quote Adler again: 'The important thing is not what one is born with, but what use one makes of that equipment.' You want to be Y or someone else because you are utterly focused on what you were born with. Instead, you've got to focus on what you can make of your equipment.

UNHAPPINESS IS SOMETHING
YOU CHOOSE FOR YOURSELF

YOUTH: No way. That's unreasonable.

PHILOSOPHER: Why is it unreasonable?

YOUTH: Why? Some people are born into affluent circumstances with parents who are nice, and others are born poor with bad parents. Because that's how the world is. And I don't really want to get into this sort of subject, but things aren't equal in the world and differences between race, nationality and ethnicity remain as deep as ever. It's only natural to focus on what you were born with. All your talk is just academic theory—you're ignoring the real world!

PHILOSOPHER: It is you who is ignoring reality. Does fixating on what you are born with change the reality? We are not replaceable machines. It is not replacement we need, but renewal.

YOUTH: To me, replacement and renewal are one and the same. You're avoiding the main point. Look, there is such a thing as unhappiness from birth. Please acknowledge that, first of all.

PHILOSOPHER: I will not acknowledge that.

YOUTH: Why?

PHILOSOPHER: For one thing, right now you are unable to feel real happiness. You find living hard, and even wish you could be reborn as a different person. But you are unhappy now because you your-self chose 'being unhappy'. Not because you were born under an unlucky star.

YOUTH: I chose to be unhappy? How can I possibly accept that?

PHILOSOPHER: There's nothing extraordinary about it. It's been repeated ever since the classical Greek era. Have you heard the saying 'no one desires evil'? It's a proposition generally known as a Socratic paradox.

YOUTH: There's no shortage of people who desire evil, is there? Of course, there are plenty of thieves and murderers, and don't forget all the politicians and officials with their shady deals. It's probably harder to find a truly good, upright person who does not desire evil.

PHILOSOPHER: Without question, there is no shortage of behaviour that is evil. But no one, not even the most hardened criminal, becomes involved in crime purely out of a desire to engage in evil acts. Every criminal has an internal justification for getting involved in crime. A dispute over money leads someone to engage in murder, for instance. To the perpetrator, it is something for which there is a justification, and which can be restated as an accomplishment of 'good'. Of course, this is not good in a moral sense, but good in the sense of being 'of benefit to oneself'.

YOUTH: Of benefit to oneself?

PHILOSOPHER: The Greek word for 'good' (*agathon*) does not have a moral meaning. It just means 'beneficial'. Conversely, the word for 'evil' (*kakon*) means 'not beneficial'. Our world is rife with injustices and misdeeds of all kinds, yet there is not one person who desires evil in the purest sense of the word; that is to say something 'not beneficial'.

YOUTH: What does this have to do with me?

PHILOSOPHER: At some stage in your life, you chose 'being unhappy'. It is not because you were born into unhappy circumstances or ended up in an unhappy situation. It's that you judged 'being unhappy' to be good for you.

YOUTH: Why? What for?

PHILOSOPHER: How do you justify this? Why did you choose to be unhappy? I have no way of knowing the specific answer or details. Perhaps it will become clearer as we debate this.

YOUTH: You are really trying to make a fool of me. You think this passes for philosophy? I do not accept this at all.

In spite of himself, the young man got up and glared at the philosopher. *I chose an unhappy life? Because it was good for me? What an absurd argument! Why is he going to such lengths to ridicule me? What did I do wrong? I'll dismantle his argument, no matter what it takes. I'll make him kneel before me.* **The young man's face flushed with excitement.**

PEOPLE ALWAYS CHOOSE
NOT TO CHANGE

PHILOSOPHER: Sit down. As things stand, it's only natural that our views clash. I will now give a simple explanation as to the manner in which humans are understood in Adlerian psychology.

YOUTH: Okay, but please be brief.

PHILOSOPHER: Earlier you said that any person's disposition or personality cannot be changed. In Adlerian psychology, we describe personality and disposition with the word 'lifestyle'.

YOUTH: Lifestyle?

PHILOSOPHER: Yes. Lifestyle is the tendencies of thought and action in life.

YOUTH: Tendencies of thought and action?

PHILOSOPHER: How one sees the world. And how one sees oneself. Think of lifestyle as a concept bringing together these ways of finding meaning. In a narrow sense, lifestyle could be defined as someone's personality; taken more broadly, it is a word that encompasses the worldview of that person and their outlook on life.

YOUTH: Their view of the world?

PHILOSOPHER: Say there's someone who worries about himself and says, 'I am a pessimist.' One could rephrase that to instead say, 'I have a pessimistic view of the world.' You could consider that the issue is not personality, but rather the view of the world. It seems that the word 'personality' is nuanced, and suggests being unchangeable. But if we're talking about a view of the world, well then, that should be possible to alter.

YOUTH: Hmm. This is kind of confusing. When you speak of a lifestyle, do you mean a 'way of living'?

PHILOSOPHER: Yes, you could put it that way. To be a little more accurate, it is 'the way one's life should be'. You probably think of disposition or personality as something with which you are endowed, without any connection to your will. In Adlerian psychology, however, lifestyle is thought of as something that you choose for yourself.

YOUTH: That you choose for yourself?

PHILOSOPHER: Yes, exactly. You choose your lifestyle.

YOUTH: So, not only did I choose to be unhappy, but I even went so far as to choose this warped personality, too?

PHILOSOPHER: Absolutely.

YOUTH: Ha! Now you're really pushing it. When I became aware, I already had this personality. I certainly don't have any recollection of having chosen it. But it's the same for you, isn't it? Being able to choose one's own personality at will . . . Now that sounds like you're talking about robots, not people.

PHILOSOPHER: Of course, you did not consciously choose 'this kind of self'. Your first choice was probably unconscious, combined with external factors you have referred to; that is, race, nationality, culture, and home environment. These certainly had a significant influence on that choice. Nevertheless, it is you who chose 'this kind of self'.

YOUTH: I don't get what you're saying. How on earth could I have chosen it?

PHILOSOPHER: Adlerian psychology's view is that it happens around the age of ten.

YOUTH: Well, for argument's sake—and now I'm really going out on a limb—say that when I was ten, I unconsciously made this choice of lifestyle or whatever. Would that even matter? You can call it personality or disposition or lifestyle, but, regardless, I had already become 'this kind of self'. The state of things doesn't change at all.

PHILOSOPHER: That is not true. If your lifestyle is not something that you were naturally born with, but something you chose yourself, then it must be possible to choose it over again.

YOUTH: Now you're saying I can choose it all over?

PHILOSOPHER: Maybe you haven't been aware of your lifestyle until now, and maybe you haven't been aware of the concept of lifestyle either. Of course, no one can choose his or her own birth. Being born in this country, in this era, and with these parents, are things you did not choose. And all these things have a great deal of influence. You'll probably face disappointment, and start looking at other people and feeling, *I wish I'd been born in their circumstances.* But you can't let it end there. The issue is not the past, but here, in the present. And now you've learned about lifestyle. But what you do with it from here on in is your responsibility. Whether you go on choosing the lifestyle you've had up till now, or you choose a new lifestyle altogether, it's entirely up to you.

YOUTH: Then how do I choose again? You're telling me, 'You chose that lifestyle yourself, so go ahead and select a new one instantly,' but there's no way I can just change on the spot!

PHILOSOPHER: Yes, you *can*. People can change at any time, regardless of the environments they are in. You are only unable to change because you are making the decision not to.

YOUTH: What do you mean, exactly?

PHILOSOPHER: People are constantly selecting their lifestyles. Right now, while we are having this tête-a-tête, we are selecting ours. You describe yourself as an unhappy person. You say that you want to change right this minute. You even claim that you want to be reborn as a different person. After all that then, why are you still unable to change? It is because you are making the persistent decision not to change your lifestyle.

YOUTH: No, don't you see that's completely illogical? I do want to change; that is my sincere wish. So, how could I be making the decision not to?

PHILOSOPHER: Although there are some small inconveniences and limitations, you probably think that the lifestyle you have now is the most practical one, and that it's just easier to leave things as they are. If you stay just like this, experience enables you to respond properly to events as they occur, while guessing the results of one's actions.

You could say it's like driving your old, familiar car. It might rattle a bit, but one can take that into account and manoeuvre easily. On the other hand, if one chooses a new lifestyle, no one can predict what might happen to the new self, or have any idea how to deal with events as they arise. It will be hard to see ahead to the future, and life will be filled with anxiety. A more painful and unhappy life might lie ahead. Simply put, people have various complaints about things, but it's easier and more secure to be just the way one is.

YOUTH: One wants to change, but changing is scary?

PHILOSOPHER: When we try to change our lifestyles, we put our great courage to the test. There is the anxiety generated by changing, and the disappointment attendant to not changing. I am sure you have selected the latter.

YOUTH: Wait . . . Just now, you used the word 'courage'.

PHILOSOPHER: Yes. Adlerian psychology is a psychology of courage. Your unhappiness cannot be blamed on your past or your environment. And it isn't that you lack competence. You just lack courage. One might say you are lacking in the courage to be happy.

YOUR LIFE IS DECIDED
HERE AND NOW

YOUTH: The courage to be happy, huh?

PHILOSOPHER: Do you need further explanation?

YOUTH: No, hold on. This is getting confusing. First, you tell me that the world is a simple place. That it only seems complicated because of me, and that my subjective view is making it that way. And also, that life just seems complicated because I make it complicated, all of which is what makes it difficult for me to live happily. Then, you say that one should take the stance of teleology, as opposed to Freudian aetiology; that one must not search for causes in one's past, and should deny trauma. You say that people act to achieve some goal or other, instead of being creatures who are driven by causes in their past. Right?

PHILOSOPHER: Yes.

YOUTH: Furthermore, as the major premise of teleology, you say that people can change. That people are always selecting their own lifestyles.

PHILOSOPHER: That is correct.

YOUTH: So, I am unable to change because I myself keep repeatedly making the decision not to change. I don't have enough courage to choose a new lifestyle. In other words, I do not have enough courage to be happy, and that's why I'm unhappy. Have I got anything wrong?

PHILOSOPHER: No, you haven't.

YOUTH: Okay, in that case, my question is, what are the real measures I should take? What do I need to do to change my life? You haven't explained all that yet.

PHILOSOPHER: You are right. What you should do now is make a decision to stop your current lifestyle. For instance, earlier you said, 'If only I could be someone like Y, I'd be happy.' As long as you live that way, in the realm of the possibility of 'if only such and such were the case', you will never be able to change. Because saying 'if only I could be like Y' is an excuse to yourself for not changing.

YOUTH: An excuse not to change?

PHILOSOPHER: Yes. I have a young friend who dreams of becoming a novelist, but who never seems to be able to complete his work. According to him, his job keeps him too busy, and he can never find enough time to write novels, and that's why he can't complete work and enter it for writing awards. But is that the real reason? No! It's actually that he wants to leave the possibility of 'I can do it if I try' open, by not committing to anything. He doesn't want to expose his work to criticism, and he certainly doesn't want to face the reality that he might produce an inferior piece of writing and face rejection. He wants to live inside that realm of possibilities, where he can say that he could do it if he only had the time, or that he could write if he just had the proper environment, and that he really does have the talent for it. In another five or ten years, he will probably start using other excuses like 'I'm not young anymore' or 'I've got a family to think about now.'

YOUTH: I can relate all too well to how he must feel.

PHILOSOPHER: He should just enter his writing for an award, and if he gets rejected, so be it. If he did, he might grow, or discover that he should pursue something different. Either way, he would be able to move on. That is what changing your current lifestyle is about. He won't get anywhere by not submitting anything.

YOUTH: But maybe his dreams will be shattered.

PHILOSOPHER: Well, I wonder. Having simple tasks—things that should be done—while continually coming up with various reasons why one can't do them sounds like a hard way to live, doesn't it? So, in the case of my friend who dreams of becoming a novelist, it is clearly the 'I', or the 'self', that is making life complicated and too difficult to live happily.

YOUTH: But . . . That's harsh. Your philosophy is too tough!

PHILOSOPHER: Indeed, it is strong medicine.

YOUTH: Strong medicine! Yes, I agree.

PHILOSOPHER: But, if you change your lifestyle—the way of giving meaning to the world and yourself—then, both your way of inter-acting with the world and your behaviour will have to change as well. Do not forget this point: one will have to change. You, just as you are, have to choose your lifestyle. It might seem hard, but it is really quite simple.

YOUTH: According to you, there's no such thing as trauma, and environment doesn't matter either. It's all just baggage, and my unhappiness is my own fault, right? I'm starting to feel I'm being criticised for everything I've ever been and done!

PHILOSOPHER: No, you are not being criticised. Rather, as Adler's teleology tells us, 'No matter what has occurred in your life up to this point, it should have no bearing at all on how you live from now on.' That you, living in the here and now, are the one who determines your own life.

YOUTH: My life is determined at this exact point?

PHILOSOPHER: Yes, because the past does not exist.

YOUTH: All right. Well, I don't agree with your theories one hundred per cent. There are many points I'm not convinced about, and that I would argue against. At the same time, your theories are worth further consideration and I'm definitely interested in learning more about Adlerian psychology. I think I've had enough for tonight, but I hope you won't mind if I come again next week. If I don't take a break, I think my head might burst.

PHILOSOPHER: I'm sure you need some time on your own to think things over. I am always here, so you can visit whenever you like. I enjoyed it. Thank you. Let's talk again.

YOUTH: Great! One last thing, if I may. Our discussion today was long and got pretty intense, and I guess I spoke rather rudely. For that, I would like to apologise.

PHILOSOPHER: Don't worry about it. You should read Plato's dialogues. The conduct and language of the disciples of Socrates are surprisingly loose. That's the way a dialogue is supposed to be.

THE
SECOND
NIGHT

*All problems are interpersonal
relationship problems*

The young man was good to his word; exactly one week later, he returned to the philosopher's study. Truth be told, he'd felt the urge to rush back there only two or three days after his first visit. He had turned things over in his mind very carefully, and his doubts had turned to certainty. In short, teleology, the attributing of the purpose of a given phenomenon, rather than its cause, was a sophistry, and the existence of trauma was beyond question. *People cannot simply forget the past, and neither can they become free from it.*

Today, the young man decided, he'd thoroughly dismantle this eccentric philosopher's theories and settle matters once and for all.

WHY YOU DISLIKE YOURSELF

YOUTH: So, after last time, I calmed myself down, focused, and thought things over. And yet, I've got to say, I still can't agree with your theories.

PHILOSOPHER: Oh? What do you find questionable about them?

YOUTH: Well, for instance, the other day I admitted that I dislike myself. No matter what I do, I can't find anything but shortcomings, and I can see no reason why I'd start liking myself. But, of course, I still want to. You explain everything as having to do with goals, but what kind of goal could I have here? I mean, what kind of advantage could there be in my not liking myself? I can't imagine there'd be a single thing to gain from it.

PHILOSOPHER: I see. You feel that you don't have any strong points; that you've got nothing but shortcomings. Whatever the facts might be, that's how you feel. In other words, your self-esteem is extremely low. So, the questions here, then, are why do you feel so wretched? And, why do you view yourself with such low esteem?

YOUTH: Because that's a fact—I really don't have any strong points.

PHILOSOPHER: You're wrong. You notice only your shortcomings because you've resolved to not start liking yourself. In order to not like yourself, you don't see your strong points, and focus only on your shortcomings. First, understand this point.

YOUTH: I have resolved to not start liking myself?

PHILOSOPHER: That's right. To you, not liking yourself is a virtue.

YOUTH: Why? What for?

PHILOSOPHER: Perhaps this is something you should think about yourself. What sort of shortcomings do you think you have?

YOUTH: I'm sure you have already noticed. First of all, there's my personality. I don't have any self-confidence, and I'm always pessimistic about everything. And I guess I'm too self-conscious, because I worry about what other people see, and, then, I live with a constant distrust of other people. I can never act naturally; there's always something theatrical about what I say and do. And it's not just my personality—there's nothing to like about my face or my body, either.

PHILOSOPHER: When you go about listing your shortcomings like that, what kind of mood does it put you in?

YOUTH: Wow, that's nasty! An unpleasant mood, naturally. I'm sure that no one would want to get involved with a guy as warped as me. If there were anyone this wretched and bothersome in my vicinity, I'd keep my distance, too.

PHILOSOPHER: I see. Well, that settles it then.

YOUTH: What do you mean?

PHILOSOPHER: It might be hard to understand from your own example, so I'll use another. I use this study for simple counselling sessions. It must have been quite a few years ago, but there was a female student who came by. She sat right where you are sitting now, in the same chair. Well, her concern was her fear of blushing. She told me that she was always turning red whenever she was out in public, and that she would do anything to rid herself of this. So I asked her, 'Well, if you *can* cure it, what will you want to do then?' And she said that there was a man she wanted. She secretly had feelings for him but wasn't ready to divulge them. Once her fear of blushing was cured, she'd confess her desire to be with him.

YOUTH: Huh! All right, it sounds like the typical thing a female student would seek counselling for. In order for her to confess her feelings for him, first she had to cure her blushing problem.

PHILOSOPHER: But is that really the whole case? I have a different opinion. Why did she get this fear of blushing? And why hadn't it gotten better? Because she needed that symptom of blushing.

YOUTH: What are you saying exactly? She was asking you to cure it, wasn't she?

PHILOSOPHER: What do you think was the scariest thing to her, the thing she wanted to avoid most of all? It was that the man would reject her, of course. The fact that her unrequited love would negate everything for her; the very existence and possibility of 'I'. This aspect is deeply present in adolescent unrequited love. But as long as she has a fear of blushing, she can go on thinking, *I can't be with him because I have this fear of blushing*. It could end without her ever working up the courage to confess her feelings to him, and she could convince herself that he would reject her anyway. And finally, she can live in the possibility that *If only my fear of blushing had gotten better, I could have . . .*

YOUTH: Okay, so she fabricated that fear of blushing as an excuse for her own inability to confess her feelings. Or maybe as a kind of insurance for when he rejected her.

PHILOSOPHER: Yes, you could put it that way.

YOUTH: Okay, that *is* an interesting interpretation. But if that were really the case, wouldn't it be impossible to do anything to help her? Since she simultaneously needs that fear of blushing, and is suffering because of it, there'd be no end to her troubles.

PHILOSOPHER: Well, this is what I told her: 'Fear of blushing is easy to cure.' She asked, 'Really?' I went on: 'But I will not cure it.' She pressed me, 'Why?' I explained, 'Look, it's thanks to your fear of blushing that you can accept your dissatisfaction with yourself and the world around you, and with a life that isn't going well. It's thanks to your fear of blushing, and it's caused by it.' She asked, 'How could it be . . . ?' I went on: 'If I did cure it, and nothing in your situation changed at all, what would you do? You'd probably come here again and say, "Give me back my fear of blushing." And that would be beyond my abilities.'

YOUTH: Hmm.

PHILOSOPHER: Her story certainly isn't unusual. Students preparing for their exams think, *If I pass, life will be rosy.* Company workers think,

If I get transferred, everything will go well. But even when those wishes are fulfilled, in many cases nothing about their situations changes at all.

YOUTH: Indeed.

PHILOSOPHER: When a client shows up requesting a cure from fear of blushing, the counsellor must not cure the symptoms. If they do, recovery is likely to be even more difficult. That is the Adlerian psychology way of thinking about this kind of thing.

YOUTH: So, what specifically do you do, then? Do you ask what they're worried about and then just leave it be?

PHILOSOPHER: She didn't have confidence in herself. She was very afraid that things being what they were, he'd reject her even if she did confess to him. And, if that happened, she'd lose even more confidence and get hurt. That's why she created the symptom of the fear of blushing. What I can do is to get the person first to accept 'myself now', and then regardless of the outcome, have the courage to step forward. In Adlerian psychology, this kind of approach is called 'encouragement'.

YOUTH: Encouragement?

PHILOSOPHER: Yes. I'll explain systematically what it consists of once our discussion has progressed a little farther. We're not at that stage yet.

YOUTH: That works for me. In the meantime, I'll keep the word 'encouragement' in mind. So, whatever happened to her?

PHILOSOPHER: Apparently, she had the chance to join a group of friends and spend time with the man, and in the end it was he who confessed his desire to be with her. Of course, she never dropped by this study again after that. I don't know what became of her fear of blushing. But she probably didn't need it any longer.

YOUTH: Yes, she clearly didn't have any use for it anymore.

PHILOSOPHER: That's right. Now, keeping this student's story in mind, let's think about your problems. You say that, at present, you notice only your shortcomings, and it's unlikely that you'll ever come to like yourself. And then, you said, 'I'm sure that no one would want to get involved with a guy as warped as me,' didn't you? I'm sure you understand this already. Why do you dislike yourself? Why do you focus only on your shortcomings, and why have you decided to not start liking yourself? It's because you are overly afraid of being disliked by other people and getting hurt in your interpersonal relationships.

YOUTH: What do you mean by that?

PHILOSOPHER: Just like the young woman with the fear of blushing, who was afraid of being rejected by the man, you are afraid of being negated by other people. You're afraid of being treated disparagingly; being refused, and sustaining deep mental wounds. You think that instead of getting entangled in such situations, it would be better if you just didn't have relations with anyone in the first place. In other words, your goal is to not get hurt in your relationships with other people.

YOUTH: Huh . . .

PHILOSOPHER: Now, how can that goal be realised? The answer is easy. Just find your shortcomings, start disliking yourself, and become someone who doesn't enter into interpersonal relationships. That way, if you can shut yourself into your own shell, you won't have to interact with anyone, and you'll even have a justification ready whenever other people snub you. That it's because of your shortcomings that you get snubbed, and if things weren't this way, you too could be loved.

YOUTH: Ha-ha! Well, you've really put me in my place now.

PHILOSOPHER: Don't be evasive. Being 'the way I am' with all these shortcomings is, for you, a precious virtue. In other words, something that's to your benefit.

YOUTH: Ouch, that hurts. What a sadist; you're diabolical! Okay, yes, it's true: I *am* afraid. I don't want to get hurt in interpersonal relationships. I'm terrified of being snubbed for who I am. It's hard to admit it, but you are right.

PHILOSOPHER: Admitting is a good attitude. But don't forget, it's basically impossible to not get hurt in your relations with other people. When you enter into interpersonal relationships, it is inevitable that to a greater or lesser extent you will get hurt, and you will hurt someone, too. Adler says, 'To get rid of one's problems, all one can do is live in the universe all alone.' But one can't do such a thing.

ALL PROBLEMS ARE INTERPERSONAL RELATIONSHIP PROBLEMS

YOUTH: Wait a minute! I'm supposed to just let that one slip by? 'To get rid of one's problems, all one can do is live in the universe all alone?' What do you mean by that? If you lived all alone, wouldn't you be horribly lonely?

PHILOSOPHER: Oh, but being alone isn't what makes you feel lonely. Loneliness is having other people and society and community around you, and having a deep sense of being excluded from them. To feel lonely, we need other people. That is to say, it is only in social contexts that a person becomes an 'individual'.

YOUTH: If you were really alone, that is, if you existed completely alone in the universe, you wouldn't be an individual and you wouldn't feel lonely, either?

PHILOSOPHER: I suppose the very concept of loneliness wouldn't even come up. You wouldn't need language, and there'd be no use for logic or commonsense, either. But such a thing is impossible. Even if you lived on an uninhabited island, you would think about someone far across the ocean. Even if you spend your nights alone, you strain your ears to hear the sound of someone's breath. As long as there is someone out there somewhere, you will be haunted by loneliness.

YOUTH: But then, you could just rephrase that as 'if one could live in the universe all alone, one's problems would go away', couldn't you?

PHILOSOPHER: In theory, yes. As Adler goes so far as to assert, 'All problems are interpersonal relationship problems.'

YOUTH: Can you say that again?

PHILOSOPHER: We can repeat it as many times as you like: all problems are interpersonal relationship problems. This is a concept that runs to the very root of Adlerian psychology. If all interpersonal relationships were gone from this world, which is to say if one were alone in the universe and all other people were gone, all manner of problems would disappear.

YOUTH: That's a lie! It's nothing more than academic sophistry.

PHILOSOPHER: Of course, we cannot do without interpersonal relationships. A human being's existence, in its very essence, assumes the existence of other human beings. Living completely separate from others is, in principle, impossible. As you are indicating, the premise 'if one could live all alone in the universe' is unsound.

YOUTH: That's not the issue I am talking about. Sure, interpersonal relationships are probably a big problem. That much I acknowledge. But to say that everything comes down to interpersonal relationship problems, now that's really an extreme position. What about the worry of being cut off from interpersonal relationships, the kind of problems that an individual agonises over as an individual; problems directed to oneself. Do you deny all that?

PHILOSOPHER: There is no such thing as worry that is completely defined by the individual; so-called internal worry does not exist.

Whatever the worry that may arise, the shadows of other people are always present.

YOUTH: But still, you're a philosopher. Human beings have loftier, greater problems than things like interpersonal relationships. What is happiness, what is freedom? And what is the meaning of life? Aren't these the themes that philosophers have been investigating ever since the ancient Greeks? And you're saying, so what? Interpersonal relationships are everything? It seems kind of pedestrian to me. It's hard to believe that a philosopher would say such things.

PHILOSOPHER: Well, then, it seems there's a need to explain things a bit more concretely.

YOUTH: Yes, please do! If you're going to tell me that you're a philosopher, then you've got to really explain things, or else this makes no sense.

PHILOSOPHER: You were so afraid of interpersonal relationships that you came to dislike yourself. You've avoided interpersonal relationships by disliking yourself.

These assertions shook the youth to his very core. The words had an undeniable truth that seemed to pierce his heart. Even so, he had to find a clear rebuttal to the statement that all the problems that people experience are interpersonal relationship problems. Adler was trivialising people's issues. *The problems I'm suffering from aren't so mundane!*

FEELINGS OF INFERIORITY ARE
SUBJECT IVE ASSUMPTIONS

PHILOSOPHER: Well, let's look at interpersonal relationships from a slightly different perspective. Are you familiar with the term 'feeling of inferiority'?

YOUTH: What a silly question. As you can surely tell from our discussion up to now, I'm just a huge blob of feelings of inferiority.

PHILOSOPHER: What are those feelings, specifically?

YOUTH: Well, for instance, if I see something in a newspaper about a person around my age, someone who's really successful, I'm always overcome with these feelings of inferiority. If someone else who's lived the same amount of time I have is so successful, then what on earth am I doing with myself? Or, when I see a friend who seems happy, before I even feel like celebrating with them, I'm filled with envy and frustration. Of course, this pimple-covered face doesn't help matters, and I've got strong feelings of inferiority when it comes to my education and occupation. And then there's my income and social standing. I guess I'm just completely riddled with feelings of inferiority.

PHILOSOPHER: I see. Incidentally, Adler is thought to be the first to use the term 'feeling of inferiority' in the kind of context in which it is spoken of today.

YOUTH: Huh, I didn't know that.

PHILOSOPHER: In Adler's native German, the word is *Minderwertigkeitsgefühl*, which means a feeling (*Gefühl*) of having less (*minder*) worth (*Wert*). So, 'feeling of inferiority' is a term that has to do with one's value judgement of oneself.

YOUTH: Value judgement?

PHILOSOPHER: It's the feeling that one has no worth, or that one is only worth so much.

YOUTH: Ah, that's a feeling I know well. That's me in a nutshell. Not a day goes by without me tormenting myself that there's no point in being alive.

PHILOSOPHER: Well, then, let's have a look at my own feelings of inferiority. When you first met me, what was your impression? In terms of physical characteristics.

YOUTH: Um, well . . .

PHILOSOPHER: There's no need to hold back. Be direct.

YOUTH: All right, I guess you were smaller than I'd imagined.

PHILOSOPHER: Thank you. I am 155 centimetres tall. Adler was apparently around the same height. There was a time—until I was right around your age, actually—when I was concerned about my height. I was sure that things would be different if I were of average height, twenty or even just ten centimetres taller. As if a more enjoyable life were waiting for me. I talked to a friend about it when I was having these feelings, and he said it was 'a bunch of nonsense', and simply dismissed it.

YOUTH: That's horrible! Some friend.

PHILOSOPHER: And then he said, 'What would you do if you got taller? You know, you've got a gift for getting people to relax.' With a man who's big and strong, it's true, it does seem he can end up intimidating people just because of his size. With someone small like me, on the other hand, people let go of their wariness. So, it made me realise that having a small build was a desirable thing both to me and to those around me. In other words, there was a transformation of values. I'm not worried about my height anymore.

YOUTH: Okay, but that's—

PHILOSOPHER: Wait until I am finished. The important thing here is that my height of 155 centimetres wasn't inferior.

YOUTH: It wasn't inferior?

PHILOSOPHER: It was not, in fact, lacking in or lesser than something. Sure, my 155 centimetres is less than the average height, and an objectively measured number. At first glance, one might think it inferior. But the issue is really what sort of meaning I attribute to that height; what sort of value I give it.

YOUTH: What does that mean?

PHILOSOPHER: My feelings about my height were all subjective feelings of inferiority, which arose entirely through my comparing myself to others. That is to say, in my interpersonal relationships.

Because if there hadn't been anyone with whom to compare myself, I wouldn't have had any occasion to think I was short. Right now, you too are suffering from various feelings of inferiority. But please understand that what you are feeling is not an objective inferiority, but a subjective feeling of inferiority. Even with an issue like height, it's all reduced to its subjectivity.

YOUTH: In other words, the feelings of inferiority we're suffering from are subjective interpretations rather than objective facts?

PHILOSOPHER: Exactly. Seeing it from my friend's point of view that I get people to relax or that I don't intimidate them—such aspects can become strong points. Of course, this is a subjective interpretation. You could even say it's an arbitrary assumption. However, there is one good thing about subjectivity: it allows you to make your own choice. Precisely because I am leaving it to subjectivity, the choice to view my height as either an advantage or disadvantage is left open to me.

YOUTH: The argument that you can choose a new lifestyle?

PHILOSOPHER: That's right. We cannot alter objective facts. But subjective interpretations can be altered as much as one likes. And we are inhabitants of a subjective world. We talked about this at the very beginning, right?

YOUTH: Yes; the well water that's eighteen degrees.

PHILOSOPHER: Now, remember the German word for a feeling of inferiority, *Minderwertigkeitsgefühl*. As I mentioned a moment ago, 'feeling of inferiority' is a term that has to do with one's value judgement of oneself. Then, what on earth could this value be? Okay, take diamonds, for instance, which are traded at a high value. Or currency. We find particular values for these things, and say that one carat is this much, that prices are such and such. But if you change your point of view, a diamond is nothing but a little stone.

YOUTH: Well, intellectually, it is.

PHILOSOPHER: In other words, value is something that's based on a social context. The value given to a one-dollar bill is not an objectively attributed value, though that might be a commonsense approach. If one considers its actual cost as printed material, the value is nowhere near a dollar. If I were the only person in this world and no one else existed, I'd probably be putting those one-dollar bills in my fireplace in wintertime. Maybe I'd be using them to blow my nose. Following exactly the same logic, there should have been no reason at all for me to worry about my height.

YOUTH: If you were the only person in this world and no one else existed?

PHILOSOPHER: Yes. The problem of value in the end brings us back to interpersonal relationships again.

YOUTH: So, this connects to what you were saying about all problems being interpersonal relationship problems?

PHILOSOPHER: Yes, that's correct.

AN INFERIORITY COMPLEX
IS AN EXCUSE

YOUTH: But can you say for sure that feelings of inferiority are really a problem of interpersonal relationships? Even the kind of person who is regarded socially as a success, who doesn't need to debase himself in relationships with other people, still has some feelings of inferiority? Even the businessman who amasses enormous wealth, the peerless beauty who is the envy of all, and the Olympic gold medallist—every one of them would be plagued by feelings of inferiority. Well, that's how it seems to me. How *should* I think about this?

PHILOSOPHER: Adler recognises that feelings of inferiority are something everyone has. There's nothing bad about feelings of inferiority themselves.

YOUTH: So, why do people have them in the first place?

PHILOSOPHER: It's probably necessary to understand this in a certain order. First of all, people enter this world as helpless beings. And people have the universal desire to escape from that helpless state. Adler called this the 'pursuit of superiority'.

YOUTH: Pursuit of superiority?

PHILOSOPHER: This is something you could think of as simply 'hoping to improve' or 'pursuing an ideal state'. For instance, a toddler learns to steady himself on both legs. He has the universal desire to learn language and to improve. And all the advancements of science throughout human history are due to this 'pursuit of superiority', too.

YOUTH: Okay. And then?

PHILOSOPHER: The counterpart of this is the feeling of inferiority. Everyone is in this 'condition of wanting to improve' that is the pursuit of superiority. One holds up various ideals or goals, and heads toward them. However, on not being able to reach one's ideals, one harbours a sense of being lesser. For instance, there are chefs who, the more inspired and accomplished they become, are forever beset with the sort of feeling of inferiority that makes them say to themselves, *I'm still not good enough*, or *I've got to bring my cooking to the next level*, and that sort of thing.

YOUTH: That's true.

PHILOSOPHER: Adler is saying that the pursuit of superiority and the feeling of inferiority are not diseases, but stimulants to normal, healthy striving and growth. If it is not used in the wrong way, the feeling of inferiority, too, can promote striving and growth.

YOUTH: The feeling of inferiority is a kind of launch pad?

PHILOSOPHER: That's right. One tries to get rid of one's feeling of inferiority, and keep moving forward. One's never satisfied with one's present situation—even if it's just a single step, one wants to make progress. One wants to be happier. There is absolutely nothing wrong with the state of this kind of feeling of inferiority. There are, however, people who lose the courage to take a single step forward, and who cannot accept the fact that the situation can be changed by making realistic efforts. People who, before even doing anything, simply give up and say things like, 'I'm not good enough anyway,' or 'Even if I tried, I wouldn't stand a chance.'

YOUTH: Well, that's true. There's no doubt about it—if the feeling of inferiority is strong, most people will become negative and say, 'I'm not good enough anyway.' Because that's what a feeling of inferiority is.

PHILOSOPHER: No, that's not a feeling of inferiority—that's an inferiority complex.

YOUTH: A complex? That's what the feeling of inferiority is, isn't it?

PHILOSOPHER: Be careful. The way the word 'complex' is used today in our country, it seems to have the same meaning as 'feeling of inferiority'. You hear people saying, 'I've got a complex about my eyelids', or 'He's got a complex about his education'; that sort of thing. This is an utter misuse of the term. At base, 'complex' refers to an abnormal mental state made up of a complicated group of emotions and ideas, and has nothing to do with the feeling of inferiority. For instance, there's Freud's Oedipus complex, which is used in the context of discussing the abnormal attraction of the child to the opposite-sex parent.

YOUTH: Yes. The nuances of abnormality are especially strong when it comes to the mother complex and the father complex.

PHILOSOPHER: For the same reason, then, it's crucial to not mix up 'feeling of inferiority' and 'inferiority complex', and to think about them as clearly separate.

YOUTH: Concretely, how are they different?

PHILOSOPHER: There is nothing particularly wrong with the feeling of inferiority itself. You understand this point now, right? As Adler says, the feeling of inferiority can be a trigger for striving and growth. For instance, if one had a feeling of inferiority with regard to one's education, and resolved to oneself, *I'm not well educated, so I'll just have to try harder than anyone else*, that would be a desirable direction. The inferiority complex, on the other hand, refers to a condition of having begun to use one's feeling of inferiority as a kind of excuse. So, one thinks to oneself, *I'm not well educated, so I can't succeed*, or *I'm not good-looking, so I can't get married*. When someone is insisting on the logic of 'A is the situation, so B cannot be done' in such a way in everyday life, that is not something that fits in the feeling of inferiority category. It is an inferiority complex.

YOUTH: No, it's a legitimate causal relationship. If you're not well educated, it takes away your chances of getting work or making it in the world. You're regarded as low on the social scale, and you can't succeed. That's not an excuse at all. It's just a cold hard fact, isn't it?

PHILOSOPHER: No, you are wrong.

YOUTH: How? Where am I wrong?

PHILOSOPHER: What you are calling a causal relationship is something that Adler explains as 'apparent cause and effect'. That is to say, you convince yourself that there is some serious causal relationship where there is none whatsoever. The other day, someone told me, 'The reason I can't get married easily is that my parents got divorced when I was a child.' From the viewpoint of Freudian aetiology (the attributing of causes), the parents' divorce was a great trauma, which connects in a clear causal relationship with one's views on marriage. Adler, however, with his stance of teleology (the attributing of purpose), rejects such arguments as 'apparent cause and effect'.

YOUTH: But even so, the reality is that having a good education makes it easier to be successful in society. I had thought you were wise to the ways of the world.

PHILOSOPHER: The real issue is how one confronts that reality. If what you are thinking is, *I'm not well educated, so I can't succeed*, then instead of *I can't succeed*, you should think, *I don't want to succeed*.

YOUTH: I don't want to succeed? What kind of reasoning is that?

PHILOSOPHER: It's simply that it's scary to take even one step forward; also, that you don't want to make realistic efforts. You don't want to change so much that you'd be willing to sacrifice the pleasures you enjoy now—for instance, the time you spend playing and engaged in hobbies. In other words, you're not equipped with the *courage* to change your lifestyle. It's easier with things just as they are now, even if you have some complaints or limitations.

BRAGGARTS HAVE FEELINGS
OF INFERIORITY

YOUTH: Maybe so, but . . .

PHILOSOPHER: Further, you harbour an inferiority complex about education and think, *I'm not well educated, so I can't succeed.* Put the other way around, the reasoning can be, *If only I were well educated, I could be really successful.*

YOUTH: Hmm, true.

PHILOSOPHER: This is the other aspect of the inferiority complex. Those who manifest their inferiority complexes in words or attitudes, who say that 'A is the situation, so B cannot be done', are implying that if only it were not for A, I'd be capable and have value.

YOUTH: If only it weren't for this, I could do it, too.

PHILOSOPHER: Yes. As Adler points out, no one is capable of putting up with having feelings of inferiority for a long period of time. Feelings of inferiority are something that everyone has, but staying in that condition is too heavy to endure forever.

YOUTH: Huh? This is getting pretty confusing.

PHILOSOPHER: Okay, let's go over things one at a time. The condition of having a feeling of inferiority is a condition of feeling some sort of lack in oneself in the present situation. So then, the question is—

YOUTH: How do you fill in the part that's missing, right?

PHILOSOPHER: Exactly. How to compensate for the part that is lacking. The healthiest way is to try to compensate through striving and growth. For instance, it could be by applying oneself to one's studies, engaging in constant training or being diligent in one's work. However, people who aren't equipped with that courage end up stepping into an inferiority complex. Again, it's thinking, *I'm not well educated, so I can't succeed*. And it's implying your capability by saying, 'If only I were well educated, I could be really successful.' That 'the real me', which just happens to be obscured right now by the matter of education, is superior.

YOUTH: No, that doesn't make sense—the second thing you're saying is beyond being a feeling of inferiority. That's really more bravado than anything else, isn't it?

PHILOSOPHER: Indeed. The inferiority complex can also develop into another special mental state.

YOUTH: And what is that?

PHILOSOPHER: I doubt you have heard much about it. It's the 'superiority complex'.

YOUTH: *Superiority* complex?

PHILOSOPHER: One is suffering from strong feelings of inferiority, and, on top of that, one doesn't have the courage to compensate through healthy modes of striving and growth. That being said, one can't tolerate the inferiority complex of thinking, *A is the situation, so*

B cannot be done. One can't accept 'one's incapable self'. At that point, the person thinks of trying to compensate in some other fashion, and looks for an easier way out.

YOUTH: What way is that?

PHILOSOPHER: It's to act as if one is indeed superior, and to indulge in a fabricated feeling of superiority.

YOUTH: A fabricated feeling of superiority?

PHILOSOPHER: A familiar example would be 'giving authority'.

YOUTH: What does that mean?

PHILOSOPHER: One makes a show of being on good terms with a powerful person (broadly speaking—it could be anyone from the leader of your school class to a famous celebrity). And by doing that, one lets it be known that one is special. Behaviours like misrepresenting one's work experience or excessive allegiance to particular brands of clothing are forms of giving authority, and probably also have aspects of the superiority complex. In each case, it isn't that the 'I' is actually superior or special. It is only that one is making the 'I' look superior by linking it to authority. In short, it's a fabricated feeling of superiority.

YOUTH: And at the base of that, there is an intense feeling of inferiority?

PHILOSOPHER: Of course. I don't know much about fashion, but I think it's advisable to think of people who wear rings with rubies and emeralds on all their fingers as having issues with feelings of inferiority, rather than issues of aesthetic sensibility. In other words, they have signs of a superiority complex.

YOUTH: Right.

PHILOSOPHER: But those who make themselves look bigger on borrowed power are essentially living according to other people's value systems—they are living other people's lives. This is a point that must be emphasised.

YOUTH: So, a superiority complex. That's a very interesting psychology. Can you give me a different example?

PHILOSOPHER: There's the kind of person who likes to boast about his achievements. Someone who clings to his past glory, and is always recounting memories of the time when his light shone brightest. Maybe you know some people like this. All such people can be said to have superiority complexes.

YOUTH: The kind of man who boasts about his achievements? Yes, it is an arrogant attitude, but he can boast because he actually is superior. You can't call that a fabricated feeling of superiority.

PHILOSOPHER: Ah, but you are wrong. Those who go so far as to boast about things out loud actually have no confidence in themselves. As Adler clearly indicates, 'The one who boasts does so only out of a feeling of inferiority.'

YOUTH: You're saying that boasting is an inverted feeling of inferiority?

PHILOSOPHER: That's right. If one really has confidence in oneself, one doesn't feel the need to boast. It's because one's feeling of inferiority is strong that one boasts. One feels the need to flaunt one's superiority all the more. There's the fear that if one doesn't do that, not a single person will accept one 'the way I am'. This is a full-blown superiority complex.

YOUTH: So, though one would think from the sound of the words that inferiority complex and superiority complex were polar opposites, in actuality they border on each other?

PHILOSOPHER: Yes, they are clearly connected. Now, there is one last example I'd like to give, a complex example that deals with boasting. It is a pattern leading to a particular feeling of superiority that manifests due to the feeling of inferiority itself becoming intensified. Concretely speaking, it's bragging about one's own misfortune.

YOUTH: Bragging about one's own misfortune?

PHILOSOPHER: The person who assumes a boasting manner when talking about his upbringing and the like; the various misfortunes that have rained down upon him. If someone should try to comfort this person, or suggest some change be made, he'll refuse the helping hand by saying, 'You don't understand how I feel.'

YOUTH: Well, there are people like that, but . . .

PHILOSOPHER: Such people try to make themselves 'special' by way of their experience of misfortune, and with the single fact of their misfortune try to place themselves above others. Take the fact that I am short, for instance. Let's say that kind-hearted people come up to me and say, 'It's nothing to worry about,' or 'Such things have nothing to do with human values.' Now, if I were to reject them and say, 'You think you know what short people go through, huh?', no one would say a thing to me anymore. I'm sure that everyone around me would start treating me just as if I were a boil about to burst, and would handle me very carefully—or, should I say, circumspectly.

YOUTH: Absolutely true.

PHILOSOPHER: By doing that, my position becomes superior to other people's, and I can become special. Quite a few people try to be a 'special being' by adopting this kind of attitude when they are sick or injured, or suffering the mental anguish of heartbreak.

YOUTH: So, they reveal their feeling of inferiority, and use it to their advantage?

PHILOSOPHER: Yes. They use their misfortune to their advantage, and try to control the other party with it. By declaring how unfortunate they are and how much they have suffered, they are trying to worry the people around them (their family and friends, for example), and to restrict their speech and behaviour, and control them. The people I was talking about at the very beginning, who shut themselves up in their rooms, frequently indulge in feelings of superiority that use misfortune to their advantage. So much so that Adler himself pointed out, 'In our culture weakness can be quite strong and powerful.'

YOUTH: So, weakness is powerful?

PHILOSOPHER: Adler says, 'In fact, if we were to ask ourselves who is the strongest person in our culture, the logical answer would be the baby. The baby rules and cannot be dominated.' The baby rules over the adults with his weakness. And it is because of this weakness that no one can control him.

YOUTH: I've never encountered that viewpoint.

PHILOSOPHER: Of course, the words of the person who has been hurt—'You don't understand how I feel'—are likely to contain a certain degree of truth. Completely understanding the feelings of the person who is suffering is something that no one is capable of. But as long as one continues to use one's misfortune to one's advantage in order to be 'special', one will always need that misfortune.

The youth and philosopher had now covered a series of discussion topics: the feeling of inferiority, the inferiority complex, and the superiority complex. Psychology keywords though they clearly were, the truths they contained differed greatly from the youth's imagined meanings. Still, something didn't feel right to him, somehow. *What is it about all this that I'm having a hard time accepting? Well, it must be the introductory part, the premise, that is giving me doubts.* The youth calmly opened his mouth to speak.

LIFE IS NOT A COMPETITION

YOUTH: But, I guess I still don't really get it.

PHILOSOPHER: Okay, ask me anything you like.

YOUTH: Adler recognises that the pursuit of superiority—one's trying to be a more superior being—is a universal desire, doesn't he? On the other hand, he's striking a note of warning with regard to excessive feelings of inferiority and superiority. It'd be easy to understand if he could renounce the pursuit of superiority—then I could accept it. What are we supposed to do?

PHILOSOPHER: Think about it this way. When we refer to the pursuit of superiority, there's a tendency to think of it as the desire to try to be superior to other people; as the desire to climb higher, even if it means kicking others down—you know, the image of ascending a stairway and pushing people out of the way to get to the top. Adler does not uphold such attitudes, of course. Rather, he's saying that on the same level playing field, there are people who are moving forward, and there are people who are moving forward behind them. Keep that image in mind. Though the distance covered and the speed of walking differ, everyone is walking equally in the same flat place. The pursuit of superiority is the mindset of taking a single step forward on one's own feet, not the mindset of competition of the sort that necessitates aiming to be greater than other people.

YOUTH: So, life is not a competition?

PHILOSOPHER: That's right. It's enough to just keep moving in a forward direction, without competing with anyone. And, of course, there is no need to compare oneself with others.

YOUTH: No, that's impossible. We'll always compare ourselves to other people, no matter what. That's exactly where our feeling of inferiority comes from, isn't it?

PHILOSOPHER: A healthy feeling of inferiority is not something that comes from comparing oneself to others, but from one's comparison with one's ideal self.

YOUTH: But . . .

PHILOSOPHER: Look, all of us are different. Gender, age, knowledge, experience, appearance—no two of us are exactly the same. Let's acknowledge in a positive manner the fact that other people are different from us. And that we are not the same, but we are equal.

YOUTH: We are not the same, but we are equal?

PHILOSOPHER: That's right. Everyone is different. Don't mix up that difference with good and bad, and superior and inferior. Whatever differences we may have, we are all equal.

YOUTH: No distinction of rank for people. Idealistically speaking, I suppose so. But aren't we trying to have an honest discussion about reality, now? Would you really say, for instance, that I, an adult, and a child who is still struggling with his arithmetic, are equal?

PHILOSOPHER: In terms of the amount of knowledge and experience, and then the amount of responsibility that can be taken, there are bound to be differences. The child might not be able to tie his shoes properly, or figure out complicated mathematical equations, or be able to take the same degree of responsibility as an adult when problems arise. However, such things shouldn't have anything to do with human values. My answer is the same. Human beings are all equal, but not the same.

YOUTH: Then, are you saying that a child should be treated like a full-grown adult?

PHILOSOPHER: No, instead of treating the child like an adult, or like a child, one must treat them like a human being. One interacts with the child with sincerity, as another human being just like oneself.

YOUTH: Let's change the question. All people are equal. They're on the same level playing field. But actually, there's a disparity here, isn't there? Those who move forward are superior, and those who pursue them from behind are inferior. So, we end up at the problem of superior and inferior, don't we?

PHILOSOPHER: No, we do not. It does not matter if one is trying to walk in front of others or walk behind them. It is as if we are moving through a flat space that has no vertical axis. We do not walk in order to compete with someone. It is in trying to progress past who one is now that there is value.

YOUTH: Have you become free from all forms of competition?

PHILOSOPHER: Of course. I do not think about gaining status or honour, and I live my life as an outsider philosopher without any connection whatsoever to worldly competition.

YOUTH: Does that mean you dropped out of competition? That you somehow accepted defeat?

PHILOSOPHER: No. I withdrew from places that are preoccupied with winning and losing. When one is trying to be oneself, competition will inevitably get in the way.

YOUTH: No way! That's a tired-out old man's argument. Young folks like me have to pull themselves up by their own bootstraps amid the tension of competition. It's because I don't have a rival running alongside me that I can't outdo myself. What's wrong with thinking of interpersonal relationships as competitive?

PHILOSOPHER: If that rival was someone you could call a comrade, it's possible that it would lead to self-improvement. But, in many cases, a competitor will not be your comrade.

YOUTH: Meaning what, exactly?

YOU'RE THE ONLY ONE WORRYING ABOUT YOUR APPEARANCE

PHILOSOPHER: Let's tie up the loose ends. At the outset, you expressed dissatisfaction with Adler's definition that all problems are interpersonal relationship problems, right? That was the basis for our discussion on feelings of inferiority.

YOUTH: Yes, that's correct. The subject of feelings of inferiority was too intense, and I was on the verge of forgetting that point. Why did you bring up the subject in the first place?

PHILOSOPHER: It is connected with the subject of competition. Please remember that. If there is competition at the core of a person's interpersonal relationships, he will not be able to escape interpersonal relationship problems or escape misfortune.

YOUTH: Why not?

PHILOSOPHER: Because at the end of a competition, there are winners and losers.

YOUTH: It's perfectly fine to have winners and losers!

PHILOSOPHER: Give some thought to it then, if it were you, specifically, who had a consciousness of being in competition with the people around you. In your relations with them, you will have no choice but to be conscious of victory or defeat. Mr A got into this famous university, Mr B found work at that big company and Mr C has hooked up with such a nice-looking woman—and you'll compare yourself to them and think, *This is all I've got.*

YOUTH: Ha-ha. That's pretty specific.

PHILOSOPHER: When one is conscious of competition and victory and defeat, it is inevitable that feelings of inferiority will arise. Because one is constantly comparing oneself to others and thinking, *I beat that person* or *I lost to that person.* The inferiority complex and the superiority complex are extensions of that. Now, what kind of being do you think the other person is to you, at that point?

YOUTH: I don't know—a rival, I guess?

PHILOSOPHER: No, not a mere rival. Before you know it, you start to see each and every person, everyone in the whole world, as your enemy.

YOUTH: My enemy?

PHILOSOPHER: You start to think that people are always looking down on you and treating you with scorn; that they're all enemies who must never be underestimated, who lie in wait for any opening and attack at the drop of a hat. In short, that the world is a terrifying place.

YOUTH: Enemies who must never be underestimated . . . That's who I'm in competition with?

PHILOSOPHER: This is what is so terrifying about competition. Even if you're not a loser, even if you're someone who keeps on winning, if you are someone who has placed himself in competition, you will never have a moment's peace. You don't want to be a loser. And you always have to keep on winning if you don't want to be a loser. You can't trust other people. The reason that so many people don't really feel happy while they're building up their success in the eyes of society is that they are living in competition. Because to them, the world is a perilous place that is overflowing with enemies.

YOUTH: I suppose so, but . . .

PHILOSOPHER: But do other people actually look at you so much? Are they really watching you around the clock, and lying in wait for the perfect moment to attack? It seems rather unlikely. A young friend of mine, when he was a teenager, used to spend a lot of time in front of the mirror arranging his hair. And once, when he was doing that, his grandmother said, 'You're the only one who's worried how you look.' He says that it got a bit easier for him to deal with life after that.

YOUTH: Hey, that's a dig at me, isn't it? Sure, maybe I do see the people around me as enemies. I'm constantly in fear of being attacked, of the arrows that could come flying at me at any moment. I always think that I'm being watched by others, that I'm being subjected to harsh judgement, and that I'm going to be attacked. And it's probably true that this is a self-conscious reaction, just like the mirror-obsessed teenager. The people of the world aren't paying attention to me. Even if I were to go walking on my hands down the street, they'd take no notice! But, I don't know. Are you saying, after all, that my feeling of inferiority is something that I chose; that has some sort of goal? That just doesn't make any sense to me.

PHILOSOPHER: And why is that?

YOUTH: I have a brother who is three years older than I am. He fits the classic image of the big brother—he always does what our parents say, he excels in his studies and in sports, and he's the very picture of diligence. And from the time I was little, I was always compared to him. He is older and more advanced, so of course I could never beat him at anything. Our parents did not care at all about such circumstances, and never gave me any sign of recognition. Whatever I did, I got treated like a child, and I was berated at every opportunity and told to be quiet. I learned to keep my feelings to myself. I've lived my life totally steeped in feelings of inferiority, and I had no choice but to be conscious of being in competition with my brother!

PHILOSOPHER: I see.

YOUTH: Sometimes I think of it like this: I'm like a gourd that grew without getting enough sun. So, it is only natural that I'm all twisted up with feelings of inferiority. If there's anyone who could grow straight in such a situation, well, I'd love to meet them!

PHILOSOPHER: I understand. I really do understand how you feel. Now, let's look at 'competition' while taking into consideration your relationship with your brother. If you didn't think with a competition orientation, with regard to your brother and your other interpersonal relationships, how would people seem to you?

YOUTH: Well, my brother is my brother, and I guess other people are another story.

PHILOSOPHER: No, they should become more positive comrades.

YOUTH: Comrades?

PHILOSOPHER: Earlier, didn't you say, 'I can't celebrate other people's happiness with all my heart'? You think of interpersonal relationships as competition; you perceive other people's happiness as 'my defeat', and that is why you can't celebrate it. However, once one is released from the schema of competition, the need to triumph over someone disappears. One is also released from the fear that says, *Maybe I will lose*. And one becomes able to celebrate other people's happiness with all one's heart. One may become able to contribute actively to other people's happiness. The person who always has the will to help another in times of need—that is someone who may properly be called your comrade.

YOUTH: Hmm.

PHILOSOPHER: Now we come to the important part. When you are able to truly feel that 'people are my comrades', your way of looking at the world will change utterly. No longer will you think of the world as a perilous place, or be plagued by needless doubts; the world will appear before you as a safe and pleasant place. And your interpersonal relationship problems will decrease dramatically.

YOUTH: What a happy person you are! But you know, that's all like a sunflower. It's the reasoning of a sunflower that is bathed in full sunshine every day, and nurtured with ample watering. A gourd grown in the dim shade doesn't do so well!

PHILOSOPHER: You are returning to aetiology (the attributing of causes) again.

YOUTH: Oh yes, I sure am!

Raised by strict parents, the youth had been oppressed and compared to his elder brother ever since childhood. None of his opinions were ever heard, and he was subjected to the violent words that he was a poor excuse for a little brother. Unable to make friends even at school, he spent all his break time alone in the library, which became his sole place of refuge. This youth who had passed his early years in such a way was truly an inhabitant of aetiology. If he had not been raised by those parents; if that elder brother had never existed; and if he had not attended that school, he could have had a brighter life. The youth had been trying to participate in the discussion as cool-headedly as possible, but now his many years of pent-up feelings came bursting out.

FROM POWER STRUGGLE TO REVENGE

YOUTH: Okay, all this talk about teleology and such is pure sophistry, and trauma definitely does exist. And people cannot break free from the past. Surely you realise that? We cannot go back to the past in a time machine. As long as the past exists as the past, we live within contexts from the past. If one were to treat the past as something that does not exist, that would be the same as negating the entire life one has led. Are you suggesting I choose such an irresponsible life?

PHILOSOPHER: It is true that one cannot use a time machine or turn back the hands of time. But what kind of meaning does one attribute to past events? This is the task that is given to 'you now'.

YOUTH: All right, so let's talk about 'now'. Last time, you said that people fabricate the emotion of anger, right? And that that is the standpoint of teleology. I still cannot accept that statement. For example, how would you explain instances of anger toward society, or anger toward government? Would you say that these, too, are emotions fabricated in order to push one's opinions?

PHILOSOPHER: Certainly, there are times when I feel indignation with regard to social problems. But I would say that rather than a sudden burst of emotion, it is indignation based on logic. There is a difference between personal anger (personal grudge) and indignation with regard to society's contradictions and injustices (righteous indignation). Personal anger soon cools. Righteous indignation, on the other hand, lasts for a long time. Anger as an expression of a personal grudge is nothing but a tool for making others submit to you.

YOUTH: You say that personal grudges and righteous indignation are different?

PHILOSOPHER: They are completely different. Because righteous indignation goes beyond one's own interests.

YOUTH: Then, I'll ask about personal grudges. Surely even you get angry sometimes—for instance, if someone hurls abuse at you for no particular reason—don't you?

PHILOSOPHER: No, I do not.

YOUTH: Come on, be honest.

PHILOSOPHER: If someone were to abuse me to my face, I would think about the person's hidden goal. Even if you are not directly abusive, when you feel genuinely angry due to another person's words or behaviour, please consider that the person is challenging you to a power struggle.

YOUTH: A power struggle?

PHILOSOPHER: For instance, a child will tease an adult with various pranks and misbehaviours. In many cases, this is something done with the goal of getting attention, and will cease just before the adult gets genuinely angry. However, if the child does not stop before the adult gets genuinely angry, then his goal is actually to get in a fight.

YOUTH: Why would he want to get in a fight?

PHILOSOPHER: He wants to win. He wants to prove his power by winning.

YOUTH: I don't really get that. Could you give me some concrete examples?

PHILOSOPHER: Let's say you and a friend have been discussing the current political situation. Before long, it turns into a heated argument, and neither of you is willing to accept any differences of opinion until finally it reaches the point where he starts engaging in personal attacks—that you're stupid, and it's because of people like you that this country doesn't change; that sort of thing.

YOUTH: But if someone said that to me, I wouldn't be able to put up with it.

PHILOSOPHER: In this case, what is the other person's goal? Is it only that he wants to discuss politics? No, it isn't. It's that he finds you unbearable, and he wants to criticise and provoke you, and make you submit through a power struggle. If you get angry at this point, the moment he has been anticipating will arrive, and the relationship will suddenly turn into a power struggle. No matter what the provocation, you must not get taken in.

YOUTH: No, there's no need to run away from it. If someone wants to start a fight, it's fine to accept it. Because it's the other guy who's at fault, anyway. You can bash his nose in, the stupid fool. With words, that is.

PHILOSOPHER: Now, let's say you take control of the quarrel. And then the other man, who was seeking to defeat you, withdraws in a sportsmanlike manner. The thing is, the power struggle doesn't end there. Having lost the dispute, he rushes onto the next stage.

YOUTH: The next stage?

PHILOSOPHER: Yes. It's the revenge stage. Though he has withdrawn for the time being, he will be scheming some revenge in another place and another form, and will reappear with an act of retaliation.

YOUTH: Like what, for instance?

PHILOSOPHER: The child oppressed by his parents will turn to delinquency. He'll stop going to school. He'll cut his wrists or engage in other acts of self-harm. In Freudian aetiology, this is regarded as simple cause and effect: the parents raised the child in this way, and that is why the child grew up to be like this. It's just like pointing out that a plant wasn't watered, so it withered. It's an interpretation that is certainly easy to understand. But Adlerian teleology does not turn a blind eye to the goal that the child is hiding. That is to say, the goal of revenge on the parents. If he becomes a delinquent, stops going to school, cuts his wrists or things like that, the parents will be upset. They'll panic and worry themselves sick over him. It is in the knowledge that this will happen that the child engages in problem behaviour. So that the current goal (revenge on the parents) can be realised, not because he is motivated by past causes (home environment).

YOUTH: He engages in problem behaviour in order to upset his parents?

PHILOSOPHER: That's right. There are probably a lot of people who feel mystified by seeing a child who cuts his wrists, and think, *Why would he do such a thing?* But try to think how the people around the child—the parents, for instance—will feel as a result of the behaviour of wrist-cutting. If you do, the goal behind the behaviour should come into view of its own accord.

YOUTH: The goal being revenge?

PHILOSOPHER: Yes. And once the interpersonal relationship reaches the revenge stage, it is almost impossible for either party to find a solution. To prevent this from happening, when one is challenged to a power struggle, one must never allow oneself to be taken in.

ADMITTING FAULT IS NOT DEFEAT

YOUTH: All right, then what should you do when you're subjected to personal attacks right to your face? Do you just grin and bear it?

PHILOSOPHER: No, the idea that you are 'bearing it' is proof that you are still stuck in the power struggle. When you are challenged to a fight, and you sense that it is a power struggle, step down from the conflict as soon as possible. Do not answer his action with a reaction. That is the only thing we can do.

YOUTH: But is it really that easy to not respond to provocation? In the first place, how would you say I should control my anger?

PHILOSOPHER: When you control your anger, you're 'bearing it', right? Instead, let's learn a way to settle things without using the emotion of anger. Because after all, anger is a tool. A means for achieving a goal.

YOUTH: That's a tough one.

PHILOSOPHER: The first thing that I want you to understand here is the fact that anger is a form of communication, and that communication is nevertheless possible without using anger. We can convey our thoughts and intentions and be accepted without any need for anger. If you learn to understand this experientially, the anger emotion will stop appearing, all on its own.

YOUTH: But what if they come at you with mistaken accusations, or make insulting comments? I shouldn't get angry even then?

PHILOSOPHER: You don't seem to understand yet. It's not that you mustn't get angry, but that there is no need to rely on the tool of anger. Irascible people do not have short tempers—it is only that they do not know that there are effective communication tools other than anger. That is why people end up saying things like 'I just snapped' or 'he flew into a rage'. We end up relying on anger to communicate.

YOUTH: Effective communication tools other than anger . . .

PHILOSOPHER: We have language. We can communicate through language. Believe in the power of language, and the language of logic.

YOUTH: Certainly, if I did not believe in that, we wouldn't be having this dialogue.

PHILOSOPHER: One more thing about power struggles. In every instance, no matter how much you might think you are right, try not to criticise the other party on that basis. This is an interpersonal relationship trap that many people fall into.

YOUTH: Why's that?

PHILOSOPHER: The moment one is convinced that 'I am right' in an interpersonal relationship, one has already stepped into a power struggle.

YOUTH: Just because you think you're right? No way, that's just blowing things all out of proportion.

PHILOSOPHER: I am right. That is to say, the other party is wrong. At that point, the focus of the discussion shifts from 'the rightness of the assertions' to 'the state of the interpersonal relationship'. In other words, the conviction that 'I am right' leads to the assumption that 'this person is wrong', and finally it becomes a contest and you are thinking, *I have to win*. It's a power struggle through and through.

YOUTH: Hmm.

PHILOSOPHER: In the first place, the rightness of one's assertions has nothing to do with winning or losing. If you think you are right, regardless of what other people's opinions might be, the matter should be closed then and there. However, many people will rush into a power struggle, and try to make others submit to them. And that is why they think of 'admitting a mistake' as 'admitting defeat'.

YOUTH: Yes, there definitely is that aspect.

PHILOSOPHER: Because of one's mindset of not wanting to lose, one is unable to admit one's mistake, the result being that one ends up choosing the wrong path. Admitting mistakes, conveying words of apology, and stepping down from power struggles—none of these things is defeat. The pursuit of superiority is not something that is carried out through competition with other people.

YOUTH: So, when you're hung up on winning and losing, you lose the ability to make the right choices?

PHILOSOPHER: Yes. It clouds your judgement, and all you can see is imminent victory or defeat. Then you turn down the wrong path. It's only when we take away the lenses of competition and winning and losing that we can begin to correct and change ourselves.

OVERCOMING THE TASKS
THAT FACE YOU IN LIFE

YOUTH: Okay, but there's still a problem. It's the statement 'all problems are interpersonal relationship problems'. I can see that the feeling of inferiority is an interpersonal relationship worry, and that it has certain effects on us. And I accept as logical the idea that life is not a competition. I cannot see other people as comrades, and somewhere inside me I think of them as enemies. This is clearly the case. But the thing I find puzzling is, why does Adler place so much importance on interpersonal relationships? Why does he go so far as to say 'all' of them?

PHILOSOPHER: The issue of interpersonal relationships is so important that no matter how broadly it is addressed, it never seems to suffice. Last time I told you, 'What you are lacking is the courage to be happy.' You remember that, right?

YOUTH: I couldn't forget it if I tried.

PHILOSOPHER: So, why do you see other people as enemies, and why can't you think of them as your comrades? It is because you have lost your courage and you are running away from your 'life tasks'.

YOUTH: My life tasks?

PHILOSOPHER: Right. This is a crucial point. In Adlerian psychology, clear objectives are laid out for human behaviour and psychology.

YOUTH: What sort of objectives?

PHILOSOPHER: First, there are two objectives for behaviour: to be self-reliant and to live in harmony with society. Then, the objectives for the psychology that supports these behaviours are the consciousness that *I have the ability* and the consciousness that *people are my comrades*.

YOUTH: Just a moment. I'm writing this down . . . There are the following two objectives for behaviour: to be self-reliant and to live in harmony with society. And there are the following two objectives for the psychology that supports these behaviours: the consciousness that *I have the ability* and the consciousness that *people are my comrades* . . . Okay, I can see that it is a crucial subject: to be self-reliant as an individual while living in harmony with people and society. It seems to tie in with everything we've been discussing.

PHILOSOPHER: And these objectives can be achieved by facing what Adler calls 'life tasks'.

YOUTH: Then, what are life tasks?

PHILOSOPHER: Let's think of the word 'life' as tracing back to childhood. During childhood, we are protected by our parents and can live without needing to work. But eventually, the time comes when one has to be self-reliant. One cannot be dependent on one's parents forever, and one has to be self-reliant mentally, of course, and self-reliant in a social sense as well, and one has to engage in some form of work—which is not limited to the narrow definition of working at a company. Furthermore, in the process of growing up, one begins to have all kinds of friend relationships. Of course, one may form a love relationship with someone that may even lead to marriage. If it does, one will start a marital relationship, and if one has children, a parent–child relationship will begin. Adler made three categories of the interpersonal relationships that arise out of these processes. He referred to them as 'tasks of work', 'tasks of friendship' and 'tasks of love', and all together as 'life tasks'.

YOUTH: Are these tasks the obligations one has as a member of society? In other words, things like labour and payment of taxes?

PHILOSOPHER: No, please think of this solely in terms of interpersonal relationships. That is, the distance and depth in one's interpersonal relationships. Adler sometimes used the expression 'three social ties' to emphasise the point.

YOUTH: The distance and depth in one's interpersonal relationships?

PHILOSOPHER: The interpersonal relationships that a single individual has no choice but to confront when attempting to live as a social being—these are the life tasks. They are indeed tasks in the sense that one has no choice but to confront them.

YOUTH: Would you be more specific?

PHILOSOPHER: First, let's look at the tasks of work. Regardless of the kind of work, there is no work that can be completed all by oneself. For instance, I am usually here in my study writing manuscripts for a book. Writing is completely autonomous work that I cannot have someone else do for me. But then there is the presence of the editor and many others, without whose assistance the work would not be realised, from the people who handle book design and printing, to the distribution and bookstore staff. Work that can be completed without the cooperation of other people is in principle unfeasible.

YOUTH: Broadly speaking, I suppose so.

PHILOSOPHER: However, considered from the viewpoint of distance and depth, interpersonal relationships of work may be said to have the lowest hurdles. Interpersonal relationships of work have the easy-to-understand common objective of obtaining good results, so people can cooperate even if they don't always get along, and to some extent they have no choice but to cooperate. And as long as a relationship is formed solely on the basis of work, it will go back to being a relationship with an outsider when working hours are over or one changes jobs.

YOUTH: Yes, so true.

PHILOSOPHER: And the ones who get tripped up in the interpersonal relationships at this stage are the people referred to as 'NEETs' [a young person not in education, employment or training] or 'shut-ins' [a person confined indoors].

YOUTH: Huh? Wait a minute! Are you saying that they don't try to work simply because they want to avoid the interpersonal relationships that are associated with work, not that they don't want to work or that they're refusing to do manual labour?

PHILOSOPHER: Putting aside the question of whether or not they are conscious of it themselves, interpersonal relationships are at the core. For example, a man sends out résumés to find work and gets interviews, only to be rejected by one company after another. It hurts his pride. He starts to wonder what the purpose in working is if he has to go through such things. Or he makes a big mistake at work. The company is going to lose a huge sum of money because of him. Feeling utterly hopeless, as if he's plunged into darkness, he can't bear the thought of coming into work the following day. None of these are examples of the work itself becoming disagreeable. What is disagreeable is being criticised or rebuked by others through the work, getting labelled as having no ability or being incompetent or unsuited to the work, and hurting the dignity of one's irreplaceable self. In other words, everything is an interpersonal relationship issue.

RED STRING AND RIGID CHAINS

YOUTH: Well, I'll save my objections for later. Next, what about the task of friendship?

PHILOSOPHER: This is a friend relationship in a broader sense, away from work, as there is none of the compulsion of the workplace. It is a relationship that is difficult to initiate or deepen.

YOUTH: Ah, you've got that right! If there's a space, like one's school or workplace, one can still build a relationship. But then it would be a superficial relationship that is limited to that space. To even attempt to initiate a personal friend relationship, or find a friend in a place outside the school or workplace, would be extremely difficult.

PHILOSOPHER: Do you have anyone who you would call a close friend?

YOUTH: I have a friend. But I'm not sure I'd call him a close friend . . .

PHILOSOPHER: It used to be the same for me. When I was in high school, I did not even try to make friends, and spent my days studying Greek and German, quietly absorbed in reading philosophy books. My mother was worried about me and went to consult my homeroom teacher. And my teacher told her, 'There's no need to worry. He's a person who doesn't need friends.' Those words were very encouraging to my mother, and to me as well.

YOUTH: A person who doesn't need friends? So, in high school you didn't have a single friend?

PHILOSOPHER: No, I did have one friend. He said, 'There's nothing really worth learning at a university,' and in the end he actually did not enter university. He went into seclusion up in the mountains for several years, and these days I hear he's working in journalism in Southeast Asia. I haven't seen him in decades, but I have the feeling that if we got together again, we'd be able to hang out just as we did back then. A lot of people think that the more friends you have the better, but I'm not so sure about that. There's no value at all in the number of friends or acquaintances you have. And this is a subject that connects with the task of love, but what we should be thinking about is the distance and depth of the relationship.

YOUTH: Will it be possible for me to make close friends?

PHILOSOPHER: Of course it will. If you change, those around you will change too. They will have no choice but to change. Adlerian psychology is a psychology for changing oneself, not a psychology for changing others. Instead of waiting for others to change or waiting for the situation to change, you take the first step forward yourself.

YOUTH: Hmm . . .

PHILOSOPHER: The fact is that you came like this to visit me in my room. And, in you, I have found a young friend.

YOUTH: I am your friend?

PHILOSOPHER: Yes, because you are. The dialogue going on here is not counselling, and we do not have a work relationship. To me, you are an irreplaceable friend. Don't you think so?

YOUTH: I'm your . . . irreplaceable friend? No, I won't think anything about that right now. Let's just keep going. What about the last one, the task of love?

PHILOSOPHER: Think of it as divided into two stages: one, what are known as love relationships; and two, relationships with family, in particular parent–child relationships. We have discussed work and friendship, but, of the three tasks, most likely it is the task of love that is the most difficult. When a friend relationship has turned into love, speech and conduct that was permitted between friends may no longer be permitted the moment they become lovers. Specifically, that would mean not permitting socialising with friends of the opposite sex, and in some cases just speaking on the telephone to someone of the opposite sex is enough to arouse jealousy. The distance is that close, and the relationship that deep.

YOUTH: Yes, I suppose it can't be helped.

PHILOSOPHER: But Adler does not accept restricting one's partner. If the person seems to be happy, one can frankly celebrate that condition. That is love. Relationships in which people restrict each other eventually fall apart.

YOUTH: Wait, that's an argument that can only lead to affirming infidelity. Because if one's partner were happily having an affair, you're saying that one should celebrate even that.

PHILOSOPHER: No, I am not affirming someone having an affair. Think about it this way: the kind of relationship that feels somehow oppressive and strained when the two people are together cannot be called love, even if there is passion. When one can think, *Whenever I am with this person, I can behave very freely*, one can really feel love. One can be in a calm and quite natural state, without having feelings of inferiority or being beset with the need to flaunt one's superiority. That is what real love is like. Restriction, on the other hand, is a manifestation of the mindset of attempting to control one's partner, and also an idea founded on a sense of distrust. Being in the same space with someone who distrusts you isn't a natural situation that one can put up with, is it? As Adler says, 'If two people want to live together on good terms, they must treat each other as equal personalities.'

YOUTH: Okay.

PHILOSOPHER: However, in love relationships and marital relationships, there is the option of separating. So, even a husband and wife who have been together for many years can separate if continuing the relationship becomes distressful. In a parent–child relationship, however, in principle this cannot be done. If romantic love is a relationship connected by red string, then the relationship between parents and children is bound in rigid chains. And a pair of small scissors is all you have. This is the difficulty of the parent–child relationship.

YOUTH: So, what can one do?

PHILOSOPHER: What I can say at this stage is: you must not run away. No matter how distressful the relationship, you must not avoid or put off dealing with it. Even if in the end you're going to cut it with scissors, first you have to face it. The worst thing to do is to just stand still with the situation as it is. It is fundamentally impossible for a person to live life completely alone, and it is only in social contexts that the person becomes an 'individual'. That is why in Adlerian psychology, self-reliance as an individual and cooperation within society are put forth as overarching objectives. Then, how can one achieve these objectives? On this point, Adler speaks of surmounting the three tasks of work, friendship and love; the tasks of the interpersonal relationships that a living person has no choice but to confront.

The youth was still struggling to grasp their true meaning.

DON'T FALL FOR THE 'LIFE-LIE'

YOUTH: Ah, it's getting confusing again. You said that I see other people as enemies and can't think of them as comrades, because I'm running away from my life tasks. What was that supposed to mean, anyway?

PHILOSOPHER: Suppose, for instance, that there is a certain Mr A whom you don't like. Because he has some flaws that are hard to forgive.

YOUTH: Ha-ha, if we're looking for people I don't like, there's no shortage of candidates.

PHILOSOPHER: But it isn't that you dislike Mr A because you can't forgive his flaws. You had the goal of taking a dislike to Mr A beforehand, and then started looking for the flaws to satisfy that goal.

YOUTH: That's ridiculous! Why would I do that?

PHILOSOPHER: So that you could avoid an interpersonal relationship with Mr A.

YOUTH: No way, that's completely out of the question. It's obvious that the order of things is backwards. He did something I didn't like, that's why. If he hadn't, I'd have no reason for taking a dislike to him.

PHILOSOPHER: No, you are wrong. It's easy to see if you think back on the example of separating from a person whom one has been in a love relationship with. In relationships between lovers or married couples, there are times when, after a certain point, one becomes exasperated with everything one's partner says or does. For instance, she doesn't care for the way he eats; his slovenly appearance at home fills her with revulsion, and even his snoring sets her off. Even though until a few months ago, none of it had ever bothered her before.

YOUTH: Yes, that sounds familiar.

PHILOSOPHER: The person feels this way because at some stage she has resolved to herself, *I want to end this relationship*, and she has been looking around for the material with which to end it. The other person hasn't changed at all. It is her own goal that has changed. Look, people are extremely selfish creatures who are capable of finding any number of flaws and shortcomings in others whenever the mood strikes them. A man of perfect character could come along, and one would have no difficulty in digging up some reason to dislike him. That's exactly why the world can become a perilous place at any time, and it's always possible to see everyone as one's enemies.

YOUTH: So, I am making up flaws in other people just so that I can avoid my life tasks, and more, so I can avoid interpersonal relationships? And I am running away by thinking of other people as my enemies?

PHILOSOPHER: That's right. Adler indicated the state of coming up with all manner of pretexts in order to avoid the life tasks, and called it the 'life-lie'.

YOUTH: Okay . . .

PHILOSOPHER: Yes, it's a severe term. One shifts one's responsibility for the situation one is currently in to someone else. One is running away from one's life tasks by saying that everything is the fault of other people, or the fault of one's environment. It's exactly the same as with the story I mentioned earlier about the female student with the fear of blushing. One lies to oneself, and one lies to the people around one, too. When you really think about it, it's a pretty severe term.

YOUTH: But how can you conclude that I am lying? You don't know anything about what kind of people I have around me, or what kind of life I lead, do you?

PHILOSOPHER: True, I don't know anything about your past. Not about your parents, or your elder brother either. I know only one thing.

YOUTH: What's that?

PHILOSOPHER: The fact that you are the one who decided your lifestyle, and no one else.

YOUTH: Argh!

PHILOSOPHER: If your lifestyle were determined by other people or your environment, it would certainly be possible to shift responsibility. But we choose our lifestyles ourselves. It's clear where the responsibility lies.

YOUTH: So, you're out to condemn me. But you're calling people liars and cowards. And saying that everyone is my responsibility.

PHILOSOPHER: You must not use the power of anger to look away. This is a very important point. Adler never discusses the life tasks or life-lies in terms of good and evil. It is not morals or good and evil that we should be discussing, but the issue of courage.

YOUTH: Courage again!

PHILOSOPHER: Yes. Even if you are avoiding your life tasks and clinging to your life-lies, it isn't because you are steeped in evil. It is not an issue to be condemned from a moralistic standpoint. It is only an issue of courage.

FROM THE PSYCHOLOGY
OF POSSESSION TO THE
PSYCHOLOGY OF PRACTICE

YOUTH: So, in the end what you're talking about is courage? That reminds me, last time you said that Adlerian psychology is a 'psychology of courage'.

PHILOSOPHER: I will add to that by saying that Adlerian psychology is not a 'psychology of possession', but a 'psychology of use'.

YOUTH: So, it's that statement: 'It's not what one is born with, but what use one makes of that equipment.'

PHILOSOPHER: That's right. Thank you for remembering it. Freudian aetiology is a psychology of possession, and eventually arrives at determinism. Adlerian psychology, on the other hand, is a psychology of use, and it is you who decides it.

YOUTH: Adlerian psychology is a psychology of courage, and at the same time it is a psychology of use . . .

PHILOSOPHER: We humans are not so fragile as to simply be at the mercy of aetiological (cause and effect) traumas. From the standpoint of teleology, we choose our lives and our lifestyles ourselves. We have the power to do that.

YOUTH: But, honestly, I do not have the confidence to overcome my inferiority complex. And you might say that that's a life-lie, but I probably won't ever be able to break free from the inferiority complex.

PHILOSOPHER: Why don't you think so?

YOUTH: Maybe what you are saying is right. Actually, I'm sure it is, and courage really is what I am lacking. I can accept the life-lie as well. I am scared of interacting with people. I don't want to get hurt in interpersonal relationships, and I want to put off my life tasks. That's why I have all these excuses ready. Yes, it's exactly as you say. But isn't what you are talking about a kind of spiritualism? All you're really saying is, 'You've lost your courage, you've got to pluck up your courage.' It's no different from the silly instructor who thinks he's giving you advice when he comes up and slaps you on the shoulder and says, 'Cheer up.' Even though the reason I'm not doing well is because I can't just cheer up!

PHILOSOPHER: So, what you are saying is that you would like me to suggest some specific steps?

YOUTH: Yes, please. I am a human being. I am not a machine. I've been told that I'm all out of courage, but I can't just get a refill of courage as if I were filling up my tank with fuel.

PHILOSOPHER: All right. But we've gone quite late again tonight, so let's continue this next time.

YOUTH: You aren't running away from it, right?

PHILOSOPHER: Of course not. Next time, we will probably discuss freedom.

YOUTH: Not courage?

PHILOSOPHER: Yes, it will be a discussion of freedom, which is essential when talking about courage. Please give some thought to the matter of what freedom is.

YOUTH: What freedom is . . . Fine. I am looking forward to next time.

THE
THIRD
NIGHT

Discard other people's tasks

Two anguished weeks later, the youth paid another visit to the philosopher's study. *What is freedom? Why can't people be free? Why can't I be free? What is the true nature of whatever it is that is constraining me?* The assignment he had been given was weighing heavily on him, but it seemed impossible to find a convincing answer. The more he thought about it, the more the youth began to notice his own lack of freedom.

DENY THE DESIRE FOR RECOGNITION

YOUTH: So, you said that today we would discuss freedom.

PHILOSOPHER: Yes. Did you have any time to think about what freedom is?

YOUTH: Yes, actually. I thought about it at great length.

PHILOSOPHER: And did you arrive at any conclusions?

YOUTH: Well, I couldn't find any answers. But I did find this—it's not my own idea, but something I came across at the library, a line from a novel by Dostoevsky: 'Money is coined freedom.' What do you think? Isn't 'coined freedom' a rather refreshing term? But seriously, I was fascinated to find this one line that drove right to the heart of this thing called money.

PHILOSOPHER: I see. Certainly, if one were to speak in a very general sense of the true nature of that which is brought about by money, one might say that is freedom. It is an astute observation, to be sure. But you wouldn't go so far as to say 'freedom therefore is money', would you?

YOUTH: It's exactly as you say. There probably is freedom that can be gained by way of money. And I'm sure that freedom is greater than we imagine. Because, in reality, all the necessities of life are dealt with through financial transactions. Does it follow, then, that if one possesses great wealth, one can be free? I don't believe that is the case; I would certainly like to believe that it is not the case, and that human values and human happiness cannot be bought with money.

PHILOSOPHER: Well, say for the moment that you have obtained financial freedom. And then, though you have gained great wealth, you have not found happiness. At that time, what problems and privations would remain for you?

YOUTH: It would be the interpersonal relationships you have been mentioning. I have thought deeply about this matter. For instance, you might be blessed by great wealth, but not have anyone who loves you; you have no comrades whom you could call friends, and you are not liked by anyone. This is a great misfortune. Another thing I can't get out of my head is the word 'bonds'. Every one of us is tangled up and writhing in these strings that we call bonds. Having to be attached to a person you don't even care for, for example, or to always watch out for your awful boss's mood swings. Imagine, if you could be released from such petty interpersonal relationships, how easy things would be! But no one can really do such a thing. Wherever we go, we are surrounded by other people, and we are social individuals, who exist in our relations to other people. No matter what we do, we cannot escape the strong rope of our interpersonal relationships. I see now that Adler's statement, 'All problems are interpersonal relationship problems,' is a great insight.

PHILOSOPHER: It is a crucial point. Let's dig a little deeper. What is it about our interpersonal relationships that is robbing us of our freedom?

YOUTH: Last time, you spoke about whether one thinks of other people as enemies or as comrades. You said that if one becomes able to see others as one's comrades, one's way of looking at the world should change as well. That certainly makes sense. I felt quite convinced the other day when I left here. But, then what happened? I gave the matter some careful thought, and I noticed that there are aspects of interpersonal relationships that can't be completely explained.

PHILOSOPHER: Like what?

YOUTH: The most obvious one is the existence of parents. I could never think of parents as enemies. During my childhood, especially, they were my greatest guardians who raised and protected me. In that regard, I am sincerely grateful. Still, my parents were strict people. I told you about this last time, that they always compared me to my older brother and refused to recognise me. And they have constantly made comments about my life, saying I should study more, not make friends with people like this or that, get into this university at the very least, get this kind of job, and so on. Their demands put a lot of pressure on me, and were certainly bonds.

PHILOSOPHER: Then, what did you end up doing?

YOUTH: It seems to me that until I started university, I was never able to ignore my parents' intentions. I was anxious, which was unpleasant, but the fact of the matter is that my wishes always seemed to end up overlapping with my parents'. My place of work I chose myself, however.

PHILOSOPHER: Now that you mention it, I haven't heard about that yet. What kind of work do you do?

YOUTH: I'm now working as a librarian at a university library. My parents wanted me to take on my father's printing plant, like my brother did. Because of this, ever since I started my current job, our relationship has been somewhat strained. If they weren't my parents, and instead were enemy-like presences in my life, I probably wouldn't have minded at all. Because no matter how much they might have tried to interfere, I could always just ignore them. But as I've said, parents to me are not enemies. Whether or not they are comrades is another matter, but, at the very least, they are not what I would call enemies. It's a relationship that is much too close to be able to just ignore their intentions.

PHILOSOPHER: When you decided which university you would go to in line with your parents' wishes, what sort of emotion did you feel with regard to your parents?

YOUTH: It's complicated. I did have feelings of resentment, but, on the other hand, there was this sense of relief, too. You know, that I could get them to recognise me if I went to that school.

PHILOSOPHER: You could get them to recognise you?

YOUTH: Come on, let's stop the roundabout leading questions. I'm sure you know what I'm referring to. It's the so-called 'desire for recognition'. It's interpersonal relationship problems in a nutshell. We human beings live in constant need of recognition from others. It is precisely because the other person is not an abhorrent enemy that one wants recognition from him, isn't it? So yes, that's right; I wanted to be recognised by my parents.

PHILOSOPHER: I see. Let's talk about one of the major premises of Adlerian psychology regarding this matter. Adlerian psychology denies the need to seek recognition from others.

YOUTH: It denies the desire for recognition?

PHILOSOPHER: There is no need to be recognised by others. Actually, one must not seek recognition. This point cannot be overstated.

YOUTH: No way! Isn't desire for recognition a truly universal desire that motivates all human beings?

DO NOT LIVE TO SATISFY THE EXPECTATIONS OF OTHERS

PHILOSOPHER: Being recognised by others is certainly something to be happy about. But it would be wrong to say that being recognised is absolutely necessary. For what does one seek recognition in the first place? Or, to put it more succinctly, why does one want to be praised by others?

YOUTH: It's simple. It's through being recognised by others that each of us can truly feel we have value. It is through recognition from others that one becomes able to wipe away one's feelings of inferiority. One learns to have confidence in oneself. Yes, it's an issue of value. I think you mentioned it last time: that the feeling of inferiority is an issue of value judgement. It's because I could never get recognition from my parents that I have lived a life tainted by feelings of inferiority.

PHILOSOPHER: Now, let's consider a familiar setting. For example, let's say you've been picking up litter around your workplace. The thing is, no one seems to notice at all. Or if they do, no one has given you any appreciation for what you've done, or even said a single word of thanks. Well, will you keep on picking up litter from now on?

YOUTH: That's a difficult situation. I suppose that if no one appreciates what I'm doing, I might stop.

PHILOSOPHER: Why?

YOUTH: Picking up litter is for everyone. If I'm rolling up my sleeves and getting it done, but I don't get a word of thanks? I guess I'd probably lose my motivation.

PHILOSOPHER: This is the danger of the desire for recognition. Why is it that people seek recognition from others? In many cases, it is due to the influence of reward-and-punishment education.

YOUTH: Reward-and-punishment education?

PHILOSOPHER: If one takes appropriate action, one receives praise. If one takes inappropriate action, one receives punishment. Adler was very critical of education by reward and punishment. It leads to mistaken lifestyles in which people think, *If no one is going to praise me, I won't take appropriate action* and *If no one is going to punish me, I'll engage in inappropriate actions, too.* You already have the goal of wanting to be praised when you start picking up litter. And if you aren't praised by anyone, you'll either be indignant, or decide that you'll never do such a thing again. Clearly, there's something wrong with this situation.

YOUTH: No! I wish you wouldn't trivialise things. I'm not arguing about education. Wanting to be recognised by people you like, to be accepted by people close to you, is a normal desire.

PHILOSOPHER: You are badly mistaken. Look, we are not living to satisfy other people's expectations.

YOUTH: What do you mean?

PHILOSOPHER: You are not living to satisfy other people's expectations, and neither am I. It is not necessary to satisfy other people's expectations.

YOUTH: That is such a self-serving argument! Are you saying one should think only about oneself and live self-righteously?

PHILOSOPHER: In the teachings of Judaism, one finds a view that goes something like this: if you are not living your life for yourself, then who is going to live it for you? You are living only your own life. When it comes to who you are living it for, of course it's you. And then, if you are not living your life for yourself, who could there be to live it instead of you? Ultimately, we live thinking about 'I'. There is no reason that we must not think that way.

YOUTH: So, you are afflicted by the poison of nihilism, after all. You say that, ultimately, we live thinking about 'I'? And that that's okay? What a wretched way of thinking!

PHILOSOPHER: It is not nihilism at all. Rather, it's the opposite. When one seeks recognition from others, and concerns oneself only with how one is judged by others, in the end, one is living other people's lives.

YOUTH: What does that mean?

PHILOSOPHER: Wishing so hard to be recognised will lead to a life of following expectations held by other people who want you to be 'this kind of person'. In other words, you throw away who you really are and live other people's lives. And please remember this: if you are not living to satisfy other people's expectations, it follows that other people are not living to satisfy your expectations. Someone might not act the way you want him to, but it doesn't do to get angry. That's only natural.

YOUTH: No, it is not! That is an argument that overturns our society from its very foundation. Look, we have the desire for recognition. But in order to receive recognition from others, first we have to recognise others ourselves. It is because one recognises other people and other systems of values that one is recognised by others. It is through this relationship of mutual recognition that our very society is built. Your argument is an abhorrent, dangerous way of thinking, which will drive human beings into isolation and lead to conflict. It's a diabolical solicitation to needlessly stir up distrust and doubt.

PHILOSOPHER: Ha-ha, you certainly have an interesting vocabulary. There's no need to raise your voice—let's think about this together. One has to get recognition, or one will suffer. If one doesn't get recognition from others and from one's parents, one won't have confidence. Can such a life be healthy? So, one could think, *God is watching, so accumulate good deeds.* But that and the nihilist view that says 'there is no God, so all evil deeds are permitted' are two sides of the same coin. Even supposing that God did not exist, and that we could not gain recognition from God, we would still have to live this life. Indeed, it is in order to overcome the nihilism of a godless world that it is necessary to deny recognition from other people.

YOUTH: I don't care for all this talk about God. Think more straight-forwardly and more plainly about the mentality of real, everyday people. What about the desire to be recognised socially, for example?

Why does a person want to climb the corporate ladder? Why does a person seek status and fame? It's the wish to be recognised as somebody important by society as a whole—it's the desire for recognition.

PHILOSOPHER: Then, if you get that recognition, would you say that you've really found happiness? Do people who have established their social status truly feel happy?

YOUTH: No, but that's . . .

PHILOSOPHER: When trying to be recognised by others, almost all people treat satisfying other people's expectations as the means to that end. And that is in accordance with the stream of thought of reward-and-punishment education that says one will be praised if one takes appropriate action. If, for example, the main point of your job turns out to be satisfying other people's expectations, then that job is going to be very hard on you. Because you'll always be worried about other people looking at you and fear their judgement, and you are repressing your 'I-ness'. It might come as a surprise to you, but almost none of my clients who come for counselling are selfish people. Rather, they are suffering trying to meet the expectations of other people, the expectations of their parents and teachers. So, in a good way, they can't behave in a self-centred fashion.

YOUTH: So, I should be selfish?

PHILOSOPHER: Do not behave without regard for others. To understand this, it is necessary to know about the idea in Adlerian psychology known as 'separation of tasks'.

YOUTH: Separation of tasks? That's a new term. Let's hear about it.

The youth's irritation had reached its peak. *Deny the desire for recognition? Don't satisfy other people's expectations? Live in a more self-centred way?* What on earth was this philosopher saying? Isn't the desire for recognition itself people's greatest motivator for associating with each other and going about the formation of society? The youth wondered, *What if this 'separation of tasks' idea doesn't win me over? I won't be able to accept this man, or Adler for that matter, for the rest of my life.*

HOW TO SEPARATE TASKS

PHILOSOPHER: Say there's a child who has a hard time studying. He doesn't pay attention in class, doesn't do his homework, and even leaves his books at school. Now, what would you do if you were his father?

YOUTH: Well, of course, I would try everything I could think of to get him to apply himself. I'd hire tutors and make him go to a study centre, even if I had to pull him by the ear to get him there. I'd say that's a parent's duty. And that's actually how I was raised myself. I wasn't allowed to eat dinner until the day's homework was done.

PHILOSOPHER: Then, let me ask another question. Did you learn to enjoy studying as a result of being made to do it in such a heavy-handed manner?

YOUTH: Unfortunately, I did not. I just took care of my studies for school and for exams in a routine way.

PHILOSOPHER: I see. All right, I will talk about this from the basic stance of Adlerian psychology. When one is confronted with the task of studying, for instance, in Adlerian psychology we consider it from the perspective of 'whose task is this?'

YOUTH: Whose task?

PHILOSOPHER: Whether the child studies or not. Whether he goes out and plays with his friends, or not. Essentially this is the child's task, not the parent's task.

YOUTH: Do you mean that it is something the child is supposed to do?

PHILOSOPHER: Simply put, yes. There would be no point if the parents studied instead of the child, would there?

YOUTH: Well, no, there wouldn't.

PHILOSOPHER: Studying is the child's task. A parent's handling of that by commanding the child to study is, in effect, an act of intruding on another person's task. One is unlikely to avert a collision in this way. We need to think with the perspective of 'whose task is this?' and continually separate one's own tasks from other people's tasks.

YOUTH: How does one go about separating them?

PHILOSOPHER: One does not intrude on other people's tasks. That's all.

YOUTH: That's all?

PHILOSOPHER: In general, all interpersonal relationship troubles are caused by intruding on other people's tasks, or having one's own tasks intruded on. Carrying out the separation of tasks is enough to change one's interpersonal relationships dramatically.

YOUTH: Hmm. I don't really get it. In the first place, how can you tell whose task it is? From my point of view, realistically speaking, getting one's child to study is the duty of the parents. Because almost no child studies just out of enjoyment, and after all is said and done, the parent is the child's guardian.

PHILOSOPHER: There is a simple way to tell whose task it is. Think, *Who ultimately is going to receive the end result brought about by the choice that is made?* When the child has made the choice of not studying, ultimately, the end result of that decision—not being able to keep up in class or to get into the preferred school, for instance—does not have to be received by the parents. Clearly, it is the child who has to receive it. In other words, studying is the child's task.

YOUTH: No, no. You're completely wrong! The parent, who is more experienced in life and also acts as a guardian, has the responsibility to urge the child to study so such situations do not arise. This is something done for the good of the child and is not an act of intruding. While studying may be the child's task, getting the child to study is the parent's task.

PHILOSOPHER: It's true that one often hears parents today using the phrase, 'It's for your own good.' But they are clearly doing so in order to fulfil their own goals, which could be their appearance in the eyes of society, their need to put on airs, or their desire for control, for example. In other words, it is not 'for your own good', but for the parents'. And it is because the child senses this deception that he rebels.

YOUTH: So, even if the child hasn't been studying at all, you're saying that, since it's his task, I should just let him be?

PHILOSOPHER: One has to pay attention. Adlerian psychology does not recommend the non-interference approach. Non-interference is the attitude of not knowing, and not even being interested in knowing what the child is doing. Instead, it is by knowing what the child is doing that one protects him. If it's studying that is the issue, one tells the child that that is his task, and one lets him know that one is ready to assist him whenever he has the urge to study. But one must not intrude on the child's task. When no requests are being made, it does not do to meddle in things.

YOUTH: Does this go beyond parent–child relationships?

PHILOSOPHER: Yes, of course. In Adlerian psychology counselling, for instance, we do not think of the client's changing or not changing as the task of the counsellor.

YOUTH: What are you saying here?

PHILOSOPHER: As a result of having received counselling, what kind of resolution does the client make? To change his lifestyle, or not. This is the client's task, and the counsellor cannot intervene.

YOUTH: No way, I can't accept such an irresponsible attitude!

PHILOSOPHER: Naturally, one gives all the assistance one possibly can. But beyond that, one doesn't intrude. There's a saying that goes, 'You can lead a horse to water, but you can't make him drink.' Please think of counselling and all other assistance provided to other people in Adlerian psychology as having that kind of stance. Forcing change while ignoring the person's intentions will only lead to an intense reaction.

YOUTH: The counsellor does not change the client's life?

PHILOSOPHER: You are the only one who can change yourself.

DISCARD OTHER PEOPLE'S TASKS

YOUTH: Then, what about with shut-ins, for example? I mean, with someone like my friend. Even then, would you say, it's the separation of tasks, don't intervene, and it has no connection to the parents?

PHILOSOPHER: Can he break out of the shut-in situation or not? Or, in what way can he break out of it? In principle, this is a task that the person has to resolve himself. It is not for the parents to intervene. Nevertheless, as they are not complete strangers, some form of assistance is probably needed. At this point, the most important thing is whether the child feels he can consult frankly with his parents when he is experiencing a dilemma, and whether they have been building enough of a trust relationship on a regular basis.

YOUTH: Then, supposing your own child had shut himself in, what would you do? Please answer this not as a philosopher, but as a parent.

PHILOSOPHER: First, I myself would think, *This is the child's task.* I would try not to intervene in his shut-in situation, and I would refrain from focusing too much attention on it. Then, I would send a message to him to the effect that I am ready to assist him whenever he is in need. In that way, the child, having sensed a change in his parent, will have no choice but to make it his own task to think about what he should do. He'll probably come and ask for assistance, and he'll probably try to work some things out on his own.

YOUTH: Could you really manage to be so cut and dried if it were your own child who'd become a shut-in?

PHILOSOPHER: A parent suffering over the relationship with his or her child will tend to think, *My child is my life.* In other words, the parent is taking on the child's task as his or her own, and is no longer able to think about anything but the child. When at last the parent notices it, the 'I' is already gone from his or her life. However, no matter how much of the burden of the child's task one carries, the child is still an independent individual. Children do not become what their parents want them to become. In their choices of university, place of employment and partner in marriage, and even in the everyday subtleties of speech and conduct, they do not act according to their parents' wishes. Naturally, the parents will worry about them, and probably want to intervene at times. But, as I said earlier, other people are not living to satisfy your expectations. Though the child is one's own, he or she is not living to satisfy one's expectations as a parent.

YOUTH: So, you have to draw the line even with family?

PHILOSOPHER: Actually, with families there is less distance, so it's all the more necessary to consciously separate the tasks.

YOUTH: That doesn't make sense. On the one hand, you're talking about love, and on the other, you're denying it. If you draw the line between yourself and other people that way, you won't be able to believe in anyone anymore!

PHILOSOPHER: Look, the act of believing is also the separation of tasks. You believe in your partner; that is your task. But how that person acts with regard to your expectations and trust is other people's tasks. When you push your wishes without having drawn that line, before you know it you're engaging in stalker-like intervention. Supposing your partner did not act as you had wished. Would you still be able to believe in that person? Would you still be able to love that person? The task of love that Adler speaks of is comprised of such questions.

YOUTH: That's difficult! That's very difficult.

PHILOSOPHER: Of course, it is. But think about it this way: intervening in other people's tasks and taking on other people's tasks turns one's life into something heavy and full of hardship. If you are leading a life of worry and suffering—which stems from interpersonal relationships—first, learn the boundary of 'from here on, that is not my task'. And discard other people's tasks. That is the first step toward lightening the load and making life simpler.

HOW TO RID YOURSELF
OF INTERPERSONAL
RELATIONSHIP PROBLEMS

YOUTH: I don't know, it just doesn't sit right with me.

PHILOSOPHER: Then, let's envision a scene in which your parents are vehemently opposing your choice of place of employment. They were in fact against it, weren't they?

YOUTH: Yes, they were. I wouldn't go so far as saying they were vehemently opposed, but they did make various snide remarks.

PHILOSOPHER: Well, let's exaggerate it and say they were vehemently opposed. Your father was ranting and raving with emotion, and your mother was protesting your decision with tears in her eyes. They absolutely do not approve of you becoming a librarian, and if you will not take on the family business like your brother has, they may very well disown you. But how to come to terms with the emotion of 'not approving' is your parents' task, not yours. It is not a problem for you to worry about.

YOUTH: Now, wait a minute. Are you saying that it doesn't matter how sad I make my parents feel?

PHILOSOPHER: That's right. It doesn't matter.

YOUTH: You've got to be joking! Could there be such a thing as a philosophy that recommends unfilial behaviour?

PHILOSOPHER: All you can do with regard to your own life is choose the best path that you believe in. On the other hand, what kind of judgement do other people pass on that choice? That is the task of other people, and is not a matter you can do anything about.

YOUTH: What another person thinks of you—if they like you or dislike you—that is that person's task, not mine. Is that what you are saying?

PHILOSOPHER: That is what separating is. You are worried about other people looking at you. You are worried about being judged by other people. That is why you are constantly craving recognition from others. Now, why are you worried about other people looking at you, anyway? Adlerian psychology has an easy answer. You haven't done the separation of tasks yet. You assume that even things that should be other people's tasks are your own. Remember the words of the grandmother: 'You're the only one who's worried how you look.' Her remark drives right to the heart of the separation of tasks. What other people think when they see your face—that is the task of other people, and is not something you have any control over.

YOUTH: As theory, I get it. To my reasoning brain, it does make sense. But my emotions can't keep up with such a high-handed argument.

PHILOSOPHER: Then, let's try another tack. Say there's a man who's distressed about the interpersonal relationships at the company where he works. He has a completely irrational boss who yells at him at every opportunity. No matter how hard he tries, his boss doesn't acknowledge his efforts and never even really listens to what he says.

YOUTH: That sounds exactly like my boss.

PHILOSOPHER: But is being acknowledged by your boss 'work' that you should think of as top priority? It isn't your job to be liked by people at the place you work. Your boss doesn't like you. And his reasons for not liking you are clearly unreasonable. But in that case, there's no need for you to get cosy with him.

YOUTH: That sounds right, but the person is my boss, right? I won't get any work done if I'm shunned by my direct superior.

PHILOSOPHER: That is Adler's life-lie again. I can't do my work because I've been shunned by my boss. It's the boss's fault that my work isn't going well. The person who says such things is bringing up the existence of the boss as an excuse for the work that doesn't go well. Much like the female student with the fear of blushing, it's actually that you need the existence of an awful boss. Because then you can say, if only I didn't have this boss, I could get more work done.

YOUTH: No, you don't know my relationship with my boss! I wish you would stop making arbitrary guesses.

PHILOSOPHER: This is a discussion that is concerned with the fundamentals of Adlerian psychology. If you are angry, nothing will sink in. You think, *I've got that boss, so I can't work.* This is complete aetiology. But it's really, *I don't want to work, so I'll create an awful boss,* or *I don't want to acknowledge my incapable self, so I'll create an awful boss.* That would be the teleological way of looking at it.

YOUTH: That's probably how it'd be framed in your stock teleology approach. But, in my case, it's different.

PHILOSOPHER: Then, supposing you had done the separation of tasks. How would things be? In other words, no matter how much your boss tries to vent his unreasonable anger at you, that is not your task. The unreasonable emotions are tasks for your boss to deal with himself. There is no need to cosy up to him, or to yield to him to the point of bowing down. You should think, *What I should do is face my own tasks in my own life without lying.*

YOUTH: But, that's . . .

PHILOSOPHER: We are all suffering in interpersonal relationships. It might be the relationship with one's parents or one's elder brother, and it might be the interpersonal relationships at one's workplace. Now, last time, you were saying that you wanted some specific steps. This is what I propose. First, one should ask 'whose task is this?' Then do the separation of tasks. Calmly delineate up to what point one's own tasks go, and from what point they become another person's tasks. And do not intervene in other people's tasks, or allow even a single person to intervene in one's own tasks. This is a specific and revolutionary viewpoint that is unique to Adlerian psychology and contains the potential to utterly change one's interpersonal relationship problems.

YOUTH: Aha. I am starting to see what you meant when you said that the topic of today's discussion was freedom.

PHILOSOPHER: That's right. We are trying to talk about freedom now.

CUT THE GORDIAN KNOT

YOUTH: I am sure that if one could understand the separation of tasks and put it into practice, one's interpersonal relationships would all at once become free. But I still can't accept it.

PHILOSOPHER: Go on. I'm listening.

YOUTH: I think that, in theory, the separation of tasks is entirely right. What other people think of me, or what sort of judgement they pass on me, is the task of other people, and is not something I can do anything about. And I should just do what I have to do in my life without lying. I'd have no problem if you said this is a life truth—that's how right I think it is. But, consider this: from an ethical or moral point of view, could it be said to be the right thing to do? That is to say, a way of living that draws boundaries between oneself and others. Because wouldn't you be brushing other people away and saying 'That's intervention!' whenever they were worried about you and asked how you're doing? It seems to me that this is something that treads on the goodwill of others.

PHILOSOPHER: Have you heard of the man known as Alexander the Great?

YOUTH: Alexander the Great? Yes, I learned about him in world history.

PHILOSOPHER: He was a Macedonian king, who lived in the fourth century before Christ. When he was advancing on the Persian kingdom of Lydia, he learned of a chariot enshrined in the acropolis. The chariot had been secured tightly to a pillar in the temple by Gordias, the former king, and there was a local legend that said, 'He who unravels this knot shall be master of Asia.' It was a tightly wound knot that many men of skill had been certain they could unbind, but no one had succeeded. Now, what do you think Alexander the Great did when he stood before this knot?

YOUTH: Well, didn't he unravel the legendary knot with ease, and go on to become the ruler of Asia?

PHILOSOPHER: No, that's not how it happened. As soon as Alexander the Great saw how tight the knot was, he pulled out his sword and sliced it in half with one stroke.

YOUTH: Wow!

PHILOSOPHER: Then, it is said that he declared, 'Destiny is not something brought about by legend, but by clearing away with one's own sword.' He had no use for the power of legend, and would forge his destiny with his sword. As you know, he then proceeded to become the great conqueror of all the territories of what is now the Middle East and western Asia. This is the famous anecdote known as the Gordian knot. And so, such intricate knots—the bonds in our interpersonal relationships—are not to be unravelled by conventional methods, but must be severed by some completely new approach. Whenever I explain the separation of tasks, I always remember the Gordian knot.

YOUTH: Well, I don't mean to contradict you, but not everyone can become Alexander the Great. Isn't it precisely because there was no one else who could have cut the knot that the anecdote portraying it as a heroic deed is still conveyed to this day? It's exactly the same with the separation of tasks. Even though one knows one can just cut through something with one's sword, one might find it rather difficult. Because when one presses forward with the separation of tasks, in the end one will have to cut ties with people. One will drive people into isolation. The separation of tasks you speak of completely ignores human emotion! How could one possibly build good interpersonal relationships with that?

PHILOSOPHER: One can build them. The separation of tasks is not the final objective for interpersonal relationships. Rather, it is the gateway.

YOUTH: The gateway?

PHILOSOPHER: For instance, when reading a book, if one brings one's face too close to it, one cannot see anything. In the same way, forming good interpersonal relationships requires a certain degree of distance. When the distance gets too small and people become stuck together, it becomes impossible to even speak to each other. But the distance must not be too great, either. Parents who scold their children too much become mentally very distant. When this happens, the child can no longer even consult the parents, and the parents can no longer give the proper assistance. One should be ready to lend a hand when needed, but not encroach on the person's territory. It is important to maintain this kind of moderate distance.

YOUTH: Is distance necessary even in the kind of relationship that parents and children have?

PHILOSOPHER: Of course. Earlier, you said that the separation of tasks is something that treads on the other person's goodwill. That is a notion that is tied to reward. It's the idea that when another person does something for you, you have to do something in return—even if that person does not want anything. Rather than responding to the goodwill, it is just being tied to reward. No matter what sort of appeal the other person might make, you are the only one who decides what you should do.

YOUTH: Reward is at the root of what I am calling 'ties'?

PHILOSOPHER: Yes. When reward is at the base of an interpersonal relationship, there's a feeling that wells up in one that says, 'I gave this much, so you should give me that much back.' This is a notion that is quite different from separation of tasks, of course. We must not seek reward, and we must not be tied to it.

YOUTH: Hmm.

PHILOSOPHER: However, there are certainly situations in which it would be easier to intervene in the tasks of another person without doing any separation of tasks. For instance, in a child-raising situation, when a child is having a hard time tying his shoes. For the busy mother, it is certainly faster to tie them than to wait for him to do it himself. But that is an intervention, and it is taking the child's task away from him. And as a result of repeating that intervention, the child will cease to learn anything, and will lose the courage to face his life tasks. As Adler says, 'Children who have not been taught to confront challenges will try to avoid all challenges.'

YOUTH: But that is such a dry way of thinking.

PHILOSOPHER: When Alexander the Great cut the Gordian knot, there were probably those who felt the same way; that the unravelling of the knot by hand had meaning, and that it was a mistake to cut it with a sword; that Alexander had misunderstood the meaning of the oracle's words. In Adlerian psychology, there are aspects that are antithetical to normal social thinking. It denies aetiology, denies trauma and adopts teleology. It treats people's problems as interpersonal relationship problems. And the not-seeking of recognition and the separation of tasks, too, are probably antithetical to normal social thinking.

YOUTH: It's impossible! I can't do it!

PHILOSOPHER: Why?

The youth was devastated by the separation of tasks that the philosopher had begun describing. When one thought of all one's problems as being in one's interpersonal relationships, the separation of tasks was effective. Just by having this viewpoint, the world would become quite simple. But there was no flesh and blood in it. It gave off no sense of one's warmth as a person. Could anyone accept such a philosophy? The youth rose from his chair and pleaded loudly.

DESIRE FOR RECOGNITION
MAKES YOU UNFREE

YOUTH: Look, I have been dissatisfied for ages. The adults of the world tell the young people, 'Do something you like to do.' And they do it with smiles on their faces as if they might actually be understanding people; as if they were on the side of the young. But it's all lip service that only comes out because those young people are complete strangers to them, and the relationship is one that is completely without any kind of responsibility. Then, parents and teachers tell us, 'Get into that school,' or 'Look for a stable occupation,' and this concrete and uninteresting instruction is not merely an intervention. It's actually that they are trying to fulfil their responsibilities. It's precisely because we are closely connected to them and they are seriously concerned about our future, that they can't say irresponsible things like 'Do something you like.' I'm sure you'd put on that understanding face too, and say to me, 'Please do something you like.' But, I won't believe such a comment from another person! It's an extremely irresponsible comment, as if one were just brushing a caterpillar off one's shoulder. And if the world crushed that caterpillar, you would say, 'It's not my task,' and walk away nonchalantly. What separation of tasks, you monster!

PHILOSOPHER: Oh goodness, you're getting all bent out of shape. So, what you are saying, in other words, is that you want someone to intervene to some extent? That you want another person to decide your path?

YOUTH: Sure, maybe I do! It's like this: it's not so difficult to judge what others expect of one, or what kind of role is being demanded of one. Living as one likes, on the other hand, is extremely difficult. What does one want? What does one want to become, and what kind of life does one want to lead? One doesn't always get such a concrete idea of things. It would be a grave mistake to think that everyone has clear-cut dreams and objectives. Don't you know that?

PHILOSOPHER: Maybe it is easier to live in such a way as to satisfy other people's expectations. Because one is entrusting one's own life to them. For example, one runs along the tracks that one's parents have laid out. Even if there are a lot of things one might object to, one will not lose one's way as long as one stays on those rails. But if one is deciding one's path oneself, it's only natural that one will get lost at times. One comes up against the wall of 'how one should live'.

YOUTH: That is what I am looking for recognition from others for. You were talking about God earlier, and if we were still living in an era when God was something people believed in, I suppose that 'God is watching' might serve as a criterion for self-discipline. If one were recognised by God, maybe one didn't need recognition from others. But that era ended a long time ago. And, in that case, one has no choice but to discipline oneself on the basis that other people are watching. To aspire to be recognised by others and live an honest life. Other people's eyes are my guide.

PHILOSOPHER: Does one choose recognition from others, or does one choose a path of freedom without recognition? It's an important question—let's think about it together. To live one's life trying to gauge other people's feelings and being worried about how they look at you. To live in such a way that other's wishes are granted. There may indeed be signposts to guide you this way, but it is a very unfree way to live. Now, why are you choosing such an unfree way to live? You are using the term 'desire for recognition', but what you are really saying is that you don't want to be disliked by anyone.

YOUTH: Who does? There's no one anywhere who'd go so far as to actually want to be disliked.

PHILOSOPHER: Exactly. It is true that there is no person who wishes to be disliked. But look at it this way: what should one do to not be disliked by anyone? There is only one answer: it is to constantly gauge other people's feelings, while swearing loyalty to all of them. If there are ten people, one must swear loyalty to all ten. When one does that, for the time being one will have succeeded in not being disliked by anyone. But at this point, there is a great contradiction looming. One swears loyalty to all ten people out of the single-minded desire to not be disliked. This is like a politician who has fallen into populism and begun to make impossible promises and accept responsibilities that are beyond him. Naturally, his lies will come to light before long. He will lose people's trust, and turn his own life into one of greater suffering. And, of course, the stress of continual lying has all kinds of consequences. Please grasp this point. If one is living in a such a way as to satisfy other people's expectations, and one is entrusting one's own life to others, that is a way of living in which one is lying to oneself, and continuing that lying to include the people around one.

YOUTH: So, one should be egocentric, and live however one pleases?

PHILOSOPHER: Separating one's tasks is not an egocentric thing. Intervening in other people's tasks is essentially an egocentric way of thinking, however. Parents force their children to study; they meddle in their life and marriage choices. That is nothing other than an egocentric way of thinking.

YOUTH: So, the child can just ignore his parent's intentions and live however he pleases?

PHILOSOPHER: There is no reason of any sort that one should not live one's life as one pleases.

YOUTH: Ha-ha! Not only are you a nihilist, you're an anarchist and a hedonist to boot. I'm past being astonished, and now I'm going to start laughing any moment.

PHILOSOPHER: An adult, who has chosen an unfree way to live, on seeing a young person living freely here and now in this moment, criticises the youth as being hedonistic; of course, this is a life-lie that comes out so that the adult can accept his own unfree life. An adult who has chosen real freedom himself will not make such comments, and will instead cheer on the will to be free.

YOUTH: All right, so what you are maintaining is that freedom is the issue? Let's get to the main point. You've been using the word 'freedom' a lot, but what does freedom mean to you, anyway? How can we be free?

WHAT REAL FREEDOM IS

PHILOSOPHER: Earlier, you acknowledged that you do not want to be disliked by anyone, and said, 'There's no one anywhere who'd go so far as to actually want to be disliked.'

YOUTH: Right.

PHILOSOPHER: Well, I'm the same way. I have no desire to be disliked by other people. I would say that 'no one would go so far as to actually want to be disliked' is a sharp insight.

YOUTH: It's a universal desire!

PHILOSOPHER: Even so, regardless of our efforts, there are people who dislike me, and people who dislike you. This, too, is a fact. When you are disliked, or feel that you are being disliked, by someone, what state of mind does it put you in?

YOUTH: Very distressed, to put it simply. I wonder why I've come to be disliked, and what I did or said that might have been offensive. I think I should have interacted with the person in a different way, and I just brood and brood over it and am ridden with guilt.

PHILOSOPHER: Not wanting to be disliked by other people. To human beings, this is an entirely natural desire, and an impulse. Kant, the giant of modern philosophy, called this desire 'inclination'.

YOUTH: Inclination?

PHILOSOPHER: Yes, it is one's instinctive desires, one's impulsive desires. Now, if one were to say that living like a stone tumbling downhill and allowing such inclinations or desires or impulses to take one wherever they will is 'freedom', one would be incorrect. To live in such a way is only to be a slave to one's desires and impulses. Real freedom is an attitude akin to pushing up one's tumbling self from below.

YOUTH: Pushing oneself up from below?

PHILOSOPHER: A stone is powerless. Once it has begun to roll downhill, it will continue to roll until released from the natural laws of gravity and inertia. But we are not stones. We are beings who are capable of resisting inclination. We can stop our tumbling selves and climb uphill. The desire for recognition is probably a natural desire. So, are you going to keep rolling downhill in order to receive recognition from others? Are you going to wear yourself down like a rolling stone, until everything is smoothed away? When all that is left is a little round ball, would that be 'the real I'? It cannot be.

YOUTH: Are you saying that resisting one's instincts and impulses is freedom?

PHILOSOPHER: As I have stated repeatedly, in Adlerian psychology, we think that all problems are interpersonal relationship problems. In other words, we seek release from interpersonal relationships. We seek to be free from interpersonal relationships. However, it is absolutely impossible to live all alone in the universe. In light of what we have discussed until now, the conclusion we reach regarding 'what is freedom?' should be clear.

YOUTH: What is it?

PHILOSOPHER: In short, that 'freedom is being disliked by other people'.

YOUTH: Huh? What was that?

PHILOSOPHER: It's that you are disliked by someone. It is proof that you are exercising your freedom and living in freedom, and a sign that you are living in accordance with your own principles.

YOUTH: But, but . . .

PHILOSOPHER: It is certainly distressful to be disliked. If possible, one would like to live without being disliked by anyone. One wants to satisfy one's desire for recognition. But conducting oneself in such a way as to not be disliked by anyone is an extremely unfree way of living, and is also impossible. There is a cost incurred when one wants to exercise one's freedom. And the cost of freedom in interpersonal relationships is that one is disliked by other people.

YOUTH: No! That's totally wrong. There is no way that could be called freedom. That's a diabolical way of thinking to coax one into evildoing.

PHILOSOPHER: You've probably been thinking of freedom as 'release from organisations'. That breaking away from your home or school, your company or your nation is freedom. However, if you were to break away from your organisation, for instance, you would not be able to gain real freedom. Unless one is unconcerned by other people's judgements, has no fear of being disliked by other people, and pays the cost that one might never be recognised, one will never be able to follow through in one's own way of living. That is to say, one will not be able to be free.

YOUTH: Be disliked by other people—is that what you are saying?

PHILOSOPHER: What I am saying is, don't be afraid of being disliked.

YOUTH: But that's—

PHILOSOPHER: I am not telling you to go so far as to live in such a way that you will be disliked, and I am not saying engage in wrongdoing. Please do not misunderstand that.

YOUTH: No. Then, let's change the question. Can people actually endure the weight of freedom? Are people that strong? To not care even if one is disliked by one's own parents—can one become so self-righteously defiant?

PHILOSOPHER: One neither prepares to be self-righteous, nor becomes defiant. One just separates tasks. There may be a person who does not think well of you, but that is not your task. And again, thinking things like, *He should like me*, or *I've done all this, so it's strange that he doesn't like me*, is the reward-oriented way of thinking of having intervened in another person's tasks. One moves forward without fearing the possibility of being disliked. One does not live as if one were rolling downhill, but instead climbs the slope that lies ahead. That is freedom for a human being. Suppose that I had two choices in front of me—a life in which all people like me, and a life in which there are people who dislike me—and I was told to choose one. I would choose the latter without a second thought. Before being concerned with what others think of me, I want to follow through with my own being. That is to say, I want to live in freedom.

YOUTH: Are you free, now?

PHILOSOPHER: Yes. I am free.

YOUTH: You do not want to be disliked, but you don't mind if you are?

PHILOSOPHER: Yes, that's right. 'Not wanting to be disliked' is probably my task, but whether or not so-and-so dislikes me is the other person's task. Even if there is a person who doesn't think well of me, I cannot intervene in that. To borrow from the proverb I mentioned earlier, naturally one would make the effort to lead a horse to water. But whether he drinks or not is that person's task.

YOUTH: That's some conclusion.

PHILOSOPHER: The courage to be happy also includes the courage to be disliked. When you have gained that courage, your interpersonal relationships will all at once change into things of lightness.

YOU HOLD THE CARDS TO INTERPERSONAL RELATIONSHIPS

YOUTH: Well, I never would have imagined I'd visit a philosopher's place to hear about being disliked.

PHILOSOPHER: I am well aware that this is not an easy thing to swallow. It will probably take some time to chew over and digest. If we go any farther with this today, I think you won't be able to keep it in your head. So, I would like to talk to you about one more thing, a personal matter that relates to the separation of tasks, and then finish up for today.

YOUTH: All right.

PHILOSOPHER: This one, too, is about relationships with parents. My relationship with my father had always been a rocky one, even when I was a child. My mother died when I was in my twenties, without us ever engaging in anything like real conversation together, and after that my relationship with my father became increasingly strained. That is, until I encountered Adlerian psychology and grasped Adler's ideas.

YOUTH: Why did you have a bad relationship with your father?

PHILOSOPHER: What I have in my memory is an image from a time when he hit me. I have no recollection of what I might have done to bring it on. I only remember hiding under a desk in an attempt to escape him, when he dragged me out and hit me hard. And not just once, but many times.

YOUTH: That fear became a trauma . . .

PHILOSOPHER: I think that until I encountered Adlerian psychology, I understood it in that kind of way. Because my father was a moody, taciturn person. But to think to myself, *He hit me that time, and that is why our relationship went bad*, is a Freudian aetiological way of thinking. The Adlerian teleology position completely reverses the cause-and-effect interpretation. That is to say, I brought out the memory of being hit because I don't want my relationship with my father to get better.

YOUTH: So, first you had the goal of not wanting your relationship with your father to get better, and not wanting to repair things between you.

PHILOSOPHER: That's right. For me, it was more convenient to not repair my relationship with my father. I could use having a father like that as an excuse for why my own life wasn't going well. That for me was a virtue. And there was also the aspect of taking revenge on a feudal father.

YOUTH: That is exactly what I wanted to ask about! Even if the cause and effect were reversed, that is to say, in your case, you were able to analyse yourself and say, 'It isn't because he hit me that I have a bad relationship with my father, but that I brought out the memory of being hit because I don't want my relationship with my father to get better,' even then, how does it actually change things? It doesn't change the fact that you were hit in childhood, right?

PHILOSOPHER: One can think from the viewpoint that it is an inter-personal relationship card. As long as I use aetiology to think, *It is because he hit me that I have a bad relationship with my father,* it would be a matter that was impossible for me to do anything about. But if I can think, *I brought out the memory of being hit because I don't want my relationship with my father to get better,* then I will be holding the card to repair relations. Because if I can just change the goal that fixes everything.

YOUTH: Does that really fix things?

PHILOSOPHER: Of course.

YOUTH: I wonder if you really feel so from the bottom of your heart. I can understand it in theory, but the feeling just doesn't sit right with me.

PHILOSOPHER: Then, it's the separation of tasks. It's true that my father and I had a complicated relationship. He was a stubborn person, and I could never imagine his feelings being able to change easily. Moreover, there was a strong possibility that he had even forgotten ever raising his hands against me. However, at the time of making my resolution to repair relations, it did not matter to me what sort of lifestyle my father had, or what he thought of me, or the kind of attitude he might adopt in response to my approach—such things didn't matter at all. Even if there were no intention to repair relations on his side, I would not mind in the least. The issue was whether or not I would resolve to do it, and I was always holding the interpersonal relationship cards.

YOUTH: You were always holding the interpersonal relationship cards?

PHILOSOPHER: Yes. Many people think that the interpersonal relationship cards are held by the other person. That is why they wonder, *How does that person feel about me?*, and end up living in such a way as to satisfy the wishes of other people. But if they can grasp the separation of tasks, they will notice that they are holding all the cards. This is a new way of thinking.

YOUTH: So, due to your changing, did your father change too?

PHILOSOPHER: I did not change in order to change my father. That is an erroneous notion of trying to manipulate another person. Even if I change, it is only 'I' who changes. I do not know what will happen to the other person as a result, and that is not an aspect I can take part in. This too is the separation of tasks. Of course, there are times when, in tandem with my change—not *due to* my change—the other person changes too. In many cases, that person will have no choice but to change. But that is not the goal, and it is certainly possible that the other person will not change. In any case, changing one's own speech and conduct as a way of manipulating other people is clearly a mistaken way of thinking.

YOUTH: One must not manipulate other people, and manipulating cannot be done.

PHILOSOPHER: When we speak of interpersonal relationships, it always seems to be two-person relationships and one's relationship to a large group that come to mind, but first it is oneself. When one is tied to the desire for recognition, the interpersonal relationship cards will always stay in the hands of other people. Does one entrust the cards of life to another person, or hold onto them oneself? Please take your time and sort through these ideas again in your own home, about the separation of tasks and about freedom. I will be waiting for you here, next time.

YOUTH: All right. I will give it some thought on my own.

PHILOSOPHER: Well, then . . .

YOUTH: Please, there is just one more thing I want to ask you.

PHILOSOPHER: What is it?

YOUTH: In the end, were you able to repair your relationship with your father?

PHILOSOPHER: Yes, of course. I think so. My father fell ill, and in the last few years of his life, it was necessary for me and my family to take care of him. Then one day, when I was taking care of him as usual, my father said, 'Thank you.' I had not known my father possessed such a word in his vocabulary, and I was astonished and felt grateful for all the days that had passed. Through the long years of my caregiving life, I had tried to do whatever I could, that is to say, I had done my best to lead my father to water. And in the end, he drank. I think he did.

YOUTH: Well, thank you very much. I will come again at the same time.

PHILOSOPHER: I had a good time. Thank you, too.

THE
FOURTH
NIGHT

*Where the centre
of the world is*

That was close—I almost fell for it! The following week, the young man called on the philosopher again, and, with an indignant expression, knocked on the door.

The idea of separating tasks is certainly a useful one. You had me completely convinced last time. But it seems like such a lonely way to live. Separating the tasks and lightening the load of one's interpersonal relations is just the same as cutting one's connection to other people. And, to top it off, you're telling me to be disliked by other people? If that's what you call freedom, then I'll choose not to be free!

INDIVIDUAL PSYCHOLOGY
AND HOLISM

PHILOSOPHER: Well, you're looking rather gloomy today.

YOUTH: You see, since we last met, I've been thinking calmly and carefully about the separation of tasks, and about freedom. I waited until my emotions had settled, and then applied my reasoning mind. But the separation of tasks just doesn't seem realistic.

PHILOSOPHER: Hmm, okay. Please go on.

YOUTH: Separating tasks is basically an idea that boils down to defining a boundary and saying, 'I am I, and you are you.' Sure, there are probably fewer interpersonal relationship problems that way. But would you really say that such a way of life is right? To me, it just seems like an extremely self-centred, misguided individualism. On my first visit here, you told me that Adlerian psychology is formally referred to as 'individual psychology'. That term had been bothering me for quite a while, but I finally figured out why: what you're calling Adlerian psychology, or individual psychology, is essentially the study of an individualism that leads people into isolation.

PHILOSOPHER: It is true that the term 'individual psychology', which Adler coined, has certain aspects that may invite misunderstanding. I will explain what I mean now. First of all, etymologically speaking, the word 'individual' has the meaning 'indivisible'.

YOUTH: Indivisible?

PHILOSOPHER: Yes. In other words, it is the smallest possible unit, and therefore cannot be broken down any further. Now, what is it exactly that cannot be divided? Adler was opposed to any kind of dualistic value system that treated the mind as separate from the body; reason as separate from emotion, or the conscious mind as separate from the unconscious mind.

YOUTH: What's the point of that?

PHILOSOPHER: For example, do you remember the story about the female student who came to me for counselling on account of her fear of blushing? Why did she develop that fear of blushing? In Adlerian psychology, physical symptoms are not regarded separately from the mind (psyche). The mind and body are viewed as one, as a whole that cannot be divided into parts. Tension in the mind can make one's arms and legs shake, or cause one's cheeks to turn red, and fear can make one's face turn white. And so on.

YOUTH: Well, sure, there are parts of the mind and body that are connected.

PHILOSOPHER: The same holds true for reason and emotion, and the conscious mind and the unconscious mind, as well. A normally cool-headed person doesn't expect to have a fit of violent emotion and start shouting at someone. We are not struck by emotions that somehow exist independently from us. Each of us is a unified whole.

YOUTH: No, that is not true. It is precisely because we have the ability to view mind and body, reason and emotion, and the conscious and the unconscious mind as clearly separate from each other, that we can gain a correct understanding of people. Isn't that a given?

PHILOSOPHER: Certainly, it is true that the mind and the body are separate things, that reason and emotion are different, and that both the conscious mind and the unconscious mind exist. That said, however, when one flies into a rage and shouts at another person, it is 'I as a whole' who is choosing to shout. One would never think of emotions that somehow exist independently—unrelated to one's intentions, as it were—as having produced that shouting voice. When one separates the 'I' from 'emotion' and thinks, *It was the emotion that made me do it*, or *The emotion got the best of me, and I couldn't help it*, such thinking quickly becomes a life-lie.

YOUTH: You're referring to the time I yelled at that waiter, aren't you?

PHILOSOPHER: Yes. This view of the human being as 'I as a whole', as an indivisible being that cannot be broken down into parts, is referred to as 'holism'.

YOUTH: Well, that's fine. But I wasn't asking you for an academic theory to provide a definition of 'individual'. Look, if you take Adlerian psychology to its logical conclusion, it's basically saying 'I am I, and you are you' and leading people toward isolation. It's saying, 'I won't interfere with you, so don't interfere with me either, and we'll both go on living however we please.' Please tell me straightforwardly what your awareness is of that point.

PHILOSOPHER: All right. All problems are interpersonal relationship problems. You have an understanding of this basic tenet of Adlerian psychology, correct?

YOUTH: Yes, I do. The idea of non-interference in interpersonal relations, that is to say, the separation of tasks, probably came about as a way to resolve those problems.

PHILOSOPHER: This is something I believe I went over last time—that forming good interpersonal relationships requires a certain degree of distance; while people who get too close end up not even being able to speak to each other, it is not good to get too far apart, either. Please do not think of the separation of tasks as something that is meant to keep other people away; instead, see it as a way of thinking with which to unravel the threads of the complex entanglement of one's interpersonal relations.

YOUTH: To unravel the threads?

PHILOSOPHER: Exactly. Right now, your threads and other people's threads are all tangled up in a confused mess, and you are looking at the world while in that condition. Red, blue, brown and green; all the colours mixing together—you think of it as 'connection'. But it is not.

YOUTH: So, then, what do you think connection is?

PHILOSOPHER: Last time, I spoke of the separation of tasks as a prescription for resolving interpersonal relationship problems. But interpersonal relationships are not something that end just because one has separated the tasks. The separating of tasks is actually the point of departure for interpersonal relations. Today, let's take the discussion deeper, so as to address how interpersonal relations as a whole are viewed in Adlerian psychology, and consider the kind of relationships we should form with others.

THE GOAL OF INTERPERSONAL
RELATIONSHIPS IS A FEELING
OF COMMUNITY

YOUTH: Okay, I have a question. Please give me a simple answer that gets straight to the heart of the matter. You said that the separating of tasks is the point of departure for interpersonal relations. Well, what is the goal of interpersonal relations?

PHILOSOPHER: To get straight to the heart of the matter, it is 'community feeling'.

YOUTH: . . . Community feeling?

PHILOSOPHER: Yes. This is a key concept in Adlerian psychology, and views on its application have been the subject of much debate. In fact, Adler's proposal of the concept of community feeling drove many people to part ways with him.

YOUTH: Well, it sounds fascinating to me. What is this concept?

PHILOSOPHER: It was the time before last, I believe, that I brought up the matter of how one sees others; that is, as enemies or as comrades. Now, take that a step deeper. If other people are our comrades, and we live surrounded by them, we should be able to find in that life our own place of 'refuge'. Moreover, in doing so, we should begin to have the desire to share with our comrades—to contribute to the community. This sense of others as comrades, this awareness of 'having one's own refuge', is called 'community feeling'.

YOUTH: But what part of this is open to debate? It seems like a completely irrefutable point.

PHILOSOPHER: The issue is community. What does it consist of? When you hear the word 'community', what images come to mind?

YOUTH: There are such frameworks as one's household, school or workplace, or local society.

PHILOSOPHER: When Adler refers to community, he goes beyond the household, school, workplace and local society, and treats it as all-inclusive, covering not only nations and all of humanity, but the entire axis of time from the past to the future—and he includes plants and animals, and even inanimate objects.

YOUTH: Huh?

PHILOSOPHER: In other words, he is espousing that community is not merely one of the pre-existing frameworks that the word might bring to mind, but is also inclusive of literally *everything*; the entire universe, from the past to the future.

YOUTH: No way. Now you've lost me. The universe? Past and future? What on earth are you talking about?

PHILOSOPHER: The majority of those who hear this have similar doubts. This is not something one can comprehend immediately. Adler himself acknowledged that the community he was espousing was 'an unattainable ideal'.

YOUTH: Ha-ha. Well that's perplexing, isn't it? How about the other way around, then? Do you really comprehend and accept this community feeling, or whatever it is, that includes the entire universe?

PHILOSOPHER: I try to. Because I feel that one cannot truly comprehend Adlerian psychology without comprehending this point.

YOUTH: Okay then!

PHILOSOPHER: As I have been saying all along, Adlerian psychology has the view that all problems are interpersonal relationship problems. Interpersonal relations are the source of unhappiness. And the opposite can be said, too—interpersonal relations are the source of happiness.

YOUTH: Indeed.

PHILOSOPHER: Furthermore, community feeling is the most important index for considering a state of interpersonal relations that is happy.

YOUTH: All right. I'd like to hear all about it.

PHILOSOPHER: Community feeling is also referred to as 'social interest', that is to say, 'interest in society'. So, now I have a question for you: do you know what society's smallest unit is, from the point of view of sociology?

YOUTH: Society's smallest unit, huh? I'd say the family.

PHILOSOPHER: No, it is 'you and I'. When there are two people, society emerges in their presence, and community emerges there too. To gain an understanding of the community feeling that Adler speaks of, it is advisable to use 'you and I' as the starting point.

YOUTH: And what do you do with that as the starting point?

PHILOSOPHER: You make the switch from attachment to self (self-interest) to concern for others (social interest).

YOUTH: Attachment to self? Concern for others? What's all that about?

WHY AM I ONLY INTERESTED IN MYSELF?

PHILOSOPHER: Well, let's consider this concretely. For purposes of clarity, in place of 'attachment to self', I will use the word 'self-centred'. In your view, someone who is self-centred is what sort of person?

YOUTH: Hmm, I guess the first thing that comes to mind is the kind of person who's like a tyrant. Someone who's domineering, has no qualms about being a nuisance to others, and only thinks about things that are to his own advantage. He thinks that the world revolves around him, and he behaves like a dictator who rules by absolute authority and force. He's the kind of person who creates an enormous amount of trouble for everyone around him. Someone who's just like Shakespeare's King Lear, a typical tyrant.

PHILOSOPHER: I see.

YOUTH: On the other hand, he wouldn't necessarily be a tyrant—one might speak of the sort of person who disturbs the harmony of a group as self-centred, too. He's someone who can't operate in a group, and prefers to act alone. He never stops to reflect on his actions, even when he's late for appointments or fails to keep his promises. In a word, he is an egotist.

PHILOSOPHER: To be sure, that is the kind of image that generally comes to mind when thinking of self-centred people. But there is another type that must be taken into account. People who are incapable of carrying out the separation of tasks, and who are obsessed with the desire for recognition are also extremely self-centred.

YOUTH: Why is that?

PHILOSOPHER: Consider the reality of the desire for recognition. How much do others pay attention to you, and what is their judgement of you? That is to say, how much do they satisfy your desire? People who are obsessed with such a desire for recognition will seem to be looking at other people, while they are actually only looking at themselves. They lack concern for others, and are concerned solely with the 'I'. Simply put, they are self-centred.

YOUTH: So, would you say that people like me, who fear being judged by others, are self-centred, too? Even though I try so hard to be mindful of others and adjust myself to them?

PHILOSOPHER: Yes. In the sense that you are concerned solely with the 'I', you are self-centred. You want to be thought well of by others, and that is why you worry about the way they look at you. That is not concern for others. It is nothing but attachment to self.

YOUTH: But . . .

PHILOSOPHER: This is something I spoke of last time. The fact that there are people who do not think well of you is proof that you are living in freedom. You might have a sense of something about this that seems self-centred. But I think you have understood this from today's discussion: a way of living in which one is constantly troubled by how one is seen by others is a self-centred lifestyle in which one's sole concern is with the 'I'.

YOUTH: Well now, that is an astounding statement!

PHILOSOPHER: Not just you, but all people who are attached to the 'I' are self-centred. And that is precisely why it is necessary to make the switch from 'attachment to self' to 'concern for others'.

YOUTH: Okay, so yes, it is true that I am always looking only at myself; that, I acknowledge. I'm constantly worried about how other people see me, but not about how I see them. If you are saying I am self-centred, there is nothing that I can say to refute that. But, think about it like this: if my life were a feature-length movie, the protagonist would certainly be this 'I', wouldn't it? Is pointing the camera at the protagonist really such a reprehensible thing?

YOU ARE NOT THE CENTRE
OF THE WORLD

PHILOSOPHER: Let's go over things in order. First of all, each of us is a member of a community, and that is where we belong. Feeling that one has one's own place of refuge within the community; feeling that 'it's okay to be here', and having a sense of belonging—these are basic human desires. Whether it is one's studies, work or friendships, or one's love or marriage, all these things are connected to one's search for places and relationships in which one can feel 'it's okay to be here'. Wouldn't you agree?

YOUTH: Ah, yes, I do! That's it exactly!

PHILOSOPHER: And the protagonist in one's life is the 'I'. There is nothing wrong with the train of thought up to this point. But the 'I' does not rule the centre of the world. While the 'I' is life's protagonist, it is never more than a member of the community and a part of the whole.

YOUTH: A part of the whole?

PHILOSOPHER: People who have concern only for themselves think that they are at the centre of the world. To such people, others are merely 'people who will do something *for* me'. They half-genuinely believe that everyone else exists to serve them, and should give precedence to their feelings.

YOUTH: Just like a prince or a princess.

PHILOSOPHER: Yes, exactly. They make a leap from being 'life's protagonist' to becoming 'the world's protagonist'. For this reason, whenever they come into contact with another person, all they can think is, *What will this person give me?* However—and this is something that does not hold true for princes and princesses—this expectation is not going to be satisfied on every occasion. Because other people are not living to satisfy your expectations.

YOUTH: Indeed.

PHILOSOPHER: Then, when those expectations are not satisfied, they become deeply disillusioned and feel as if they have been horribly insulted. And they become resentful, and think, *That person didn't do anything for me*; *That person let me down*; *That person isn't my comrade anymore. He's my enemy.* People who hold the belief that they are the centre of the world always end up losing their comrades before long.

YOUTH: That's strange. Didn't you say that we are living in a subjective world? As long as the world is a subjective space, I am the only one who can be at its centre. I won't let anyone else be there.

PHILOSOPHER: I think that when you speak of 'the world', what you have in mind is something like a map of the world.

YOUTH: A map of the world? What are you talking about?

PHILOSOPHER: For example, on the map of the world used in France, the Americas are located on the left side, and Asia on the right. Europe and France are depicted at the centre of the map, of course.

The map of the world used in China, on the other hand, shows the Americas on the right side, and Europe on the left. French people who see the Chinese map of the world will most likely experience a difficult-to-describe sense of incongruity, as if they have been driven unjustly to the fringes, or cut out of the world arbitrarily.

YOUTH: Yes, I see your point.

PHILOSOPHER: But what happens when a globe is used to represent the world? Because with a globe, you can look at the world with France at the centre, or China, or Brazil for that matter. Every place is central, and no place is, at the same time. The globe may be dotted with an infinite number of centres, in accordance with the viewer's location and angle of view. That is the nature of a globe.

YOUTH: Hmm, that is true.

PHILOSOPHER: Think of what I said earlier—that you are not the centre of the world — as being the same thing. You are a part of a community, not its centre.

YOUTH: I am not the centre of the world. Our world is a globe, not a map that has been cut out on a plane. Well, I can understand that in theory, anyway. But why do I have to be aware of the fact that I'm not the centre of the world?

PHILOSOPHER: Now we will go back to where we started. All of us are searching for the sense of belonging that 'it's okay to be here'. In Adlerian psychology, however, a sense of belonging is something that one can attain only by making an active commitment to the community of one's own accord, and not simply by being here.

YOUTH: By making an active commitment? What does one do, exactly?

PHILOSOPHER: One faces one's life tasks. In other words, one takes steps forward on one's own, without avoiding the tasks of the interpersonal relations of work, friendship and love. If you are 'the centre of the world', you will have no thoughts whatsoever regarding commitment to the community; because everyone else is 'someone who will do something for me', and there is no need for you to do things yourself. But you are not the centre of the world, and neither am I. One has to stand on one's own two feet, and take one's own steps forward with the tasks of interpersonal relations. One needs to think not *What will this person give me?* but, rather, *What can I give to this person?* That is commitment to the community.

YOUTH: It is because one gives something that one can find one's refuge?

PHILOSOPHER: That's right. A sense of belonging is something that one acquires through one's own efforts—it is not something one is endowed with at birth. Community feeling is the much-debated key concept of Adlerian psychology.

It was certainly a concept that the young man found difficult to accept at first. And naturally, it upset him to be told he was self-centred. But what he found harder to accept than anything else was the incredible extent of that community, which included the universe and inanimate objects. What were Adler and this philosopher talking about, anyway? With a bewildered expression, the young man slowly opened his mouth to speak.

LISTEN TO THE VOICE OF A
LARGER COMMUNITY

YOUTH: I must admit, you're starting to lose me. Let me try to straighten things out a bit. First, at the gateway of interpersonal relations, we've got the separation of tasks, and as the goal, there's community feeling. And you're saying that community feeling is having 'a sense of others as comrades', and 'an awareness of having one's own refuge' within the community. Up to this point, it is something I can understand and accept. But the details still seem a bit far-fetched. For one thing, what do you mean by expanding this thing you call 'community' to include the entire universe, and then even the past and the future, and everything from living things to inanimate objects?

PHILOSOPHER: It certainly does make things more difficult to understand if one takes Adler's concept of community verbatim and tries to actually imagine it including the universe and inanimate objects. For the time being, suffice it to say that the scope of community is infinite.

YOUTH: Infinite?

PHILOSOPHER: Take, for example, a man who, on reaching retirement age and stopping work, quickly loses his vitality and becomes depressed. Abruptly cut off from the company that was his community and bereft of title or profession, he becomes an 'ordinary nobody'. As he is unable to accept the fact that he is now 'normal', he becomes old practically overnight. But all that really happened to the man is that he was cut off from the small community that is his company. Each person belongs to a separate community. And when it comes down to it, all of us belong to the community of the earth, and the community of the universe.

YOUTH: That's pure sophistry! To suddenly come out with 'you belong to the universe', as if that could give someone a sense of belonging.

PHILOSOPHER: It's true, there's no way one can just imagine the entire universe all of a sudden. Even so, I would like you to gain the awareness that you belong to a separate, larger community that is beyond the one you see in your immediate vicinity—for example, the country or local society in which you live—and that you are contributing in some way within that community.

YOUTH: Then, what about in a situation like this? Say there's a guy who's unmarried, has lost his job and his friends, and who avoids the company of other people and just lives off the money his parents left him. So, he's basically running away from all the tasks of work, and tasks of friendship and tasks of love. Would you say that even a guy like that belongs to some sort of community?

PHILOSOPHER: Of course. Say he goes out to buy a loaf of bread. He pays for it with a coin. That coin does not simply go back to the bakers of the bread. It goes to the producers of flour and butter; to the people who deliver those ingredients; to the purveyors of the gasoline used by the delivery vehicles; to people in the oil-producing countries where that fuel comes from, and so on. So, it's all connected. People are never truly alone or separate from community, and cannot be.

YOUTH: So, you're saying I should fantasise more when I buy bread?

PHILOSOPHER: It is not fantasy. It is fact. The community Adler speaks of goes beyond things we can see, like our households and societies, to include those connections that we cannot see.

YOUTH: Excuse me for saying so, but you're escaping into abstract theory. The issue we should be addressing here is the sense of belonging, that 'it's okay to be here'. And then, with regard to the meaning of this sense of belonging, it is the community we can see that is stronger. You will agree with that, won't you? For example, if we compare the 'company' community with the 'earth' community, the sense of belonging of someone who says 'I am a member of this company' would be stronger. To borrow your terminology, the distance and depth of the interpersonal relations are completely different. It's only natural that when we search for a sense of belonging, we will be attracted to the smaller community.

PHILOSOPHER: That is a perceptive observation. So, let's starting thinking about why we should be aware of multiple and larger communities. As I stated earlier, all of us belong to multiple communities. We belong to our households, our schools, our workplaces and the local societies and the countries in which we live. This far you agree with, yes?

YOUTH: Yes, I do.

PHILOSOPHER: Well, suppose that you, as a student, regarded the community that is 'school' as absolute. In other words, school is everything to you, your 'I' exists because of school, and no other 'I' is possible without it. But naturally, there will be occasions within that community when you run into adversity. It could be getting bullied, or not being able to make friends or keep up with your schoolwork, or not adapting to the system of the school in the first place. That is to say, it's possible that with regard to the community that is your school, you won't have that 'it's okay to be here' sense of belonging.

YOUTH: Yes, absolutely. That's quite possible.

PHILOSOPHER: When that happens, if you are thinking of school as being everything to you, you will end up without a sense of belonging to anything. And then, you will escape within a smaller community such as your home. You will shut yourself in, and maybe even turn to violence against members of your own family. And by doing such things, you will be attempting to gain a sense of belonging somehow. What I would like you to focus on here, though, is that there is 'a more separate community' and, moreover, that there is 'a larger community'.

YOUTH: What does that mean?

PHILOSOPHER: That there is a larger world that extends far beyond the confines of the school. And every one of us is a member of that world. If there is no place of refuge in your school, you should find a different refuge outside the walls of the school. You can change schools, and it's fine to withdraw from school, too. A community that you can break relations with by simply submitting a withdrawal notice is one that you can have only so much connection to, in any case. Once you know how big the world is, you will see that all the hardship you went through in school was a storm in a teacup. The moment you leave the teacup, that raging storm will be gone, and a gentle breeze will greet you in its place.

YOUTH: Are you saying that as long as you keep yourself shut up inside the teacup, you'll never stand a chance outside it?

PHILOSOPHER: Secluding yourself in your room is akin to staying in the teacup, as if you are hunkering down in a small shelter. You might be able to wait out the rain for a short while, but the storm will continue unabated.

YOUTH: Well, maybe in theory, anyway. But it's hard to break out. The decision to withdraw from school itself isn't something to be taken lightly.

PHILOSOPHER: I am sure you are right—it would not be easy. Therefore, there is a principle of action that I would like you to commit to memory. When we run into difficulties in our interpersonal relations, or when we can no longer see a way out, what we should consider first and foremost is the principle that says 'listen to the voice of the larger community'.

YOUTH: The voice of the larger community?

PHILOSOPHER: If it is a school, one does not judge things with the commonsense of the community that is the school, but instead follows the commonsense of a larger community. Now, let's say it's your school, and your teacher has been behaving in an authoritarian manner. But the power or authority your teacher wields is nothing more than an aspect of the commonsense that operates only within the small community that is the school. From the standpoint of the community that is 'human society', both you and your teacher are equal humans. If unreasonable demands are being thrust on you, it is fine to object to them directly.

YOUTH: But, it will be very difficult to object when the teacher is right in front of me.

PHILOSOPHER: Not at all. Though this might be termed a 'you and I' relationship, if it is one that can break down just because you raise an objection, then it is not the sort of relationship you need to get into in the first place. It is fine to just let go of it. Living in fear of one's relationships falling apart is an unfree way to live, in which one is living for other people.

YOUTH: You're saying to choose freedom at the same time that I have community feeling?

PHILOSOPHER: Yes, of course. Do not cling to the small community right in front of you. There will always be more 'you and I', and more 'everyone', and larger communities that exist.

DO NOT REBUKE OR PRAISE

YOUTH: Well, all right. But don't you see? You haven't touched on the essential point; that is, the course of progression from the separation of tasks to community feeling. So, first, I separate the tasks. I think of my tasks as being up to this point; and everything beyond that is other people's tasks. I don't intervene in other people's tasks, and I draw a line so that other people won't intervene in mine. But how can one build interpersonal relations with this separation of tasks, and arrive in the end at the community feeling that 'it's okay to be here'? How does Adlerian psychology advise us to overcome the life tasks of work, friendship and love? It seems like you're just trying to confuse me with abstract words, without going into any concrete explanation.

PHILOSOPHER: Yes, you've hit on the important point. How does carrying out the separating of tasks connect with good relations? That is to say, how does it connect with building the kind of relations in which we cooperate and act in harmony with each other? Which brings us to the concept of 'horizontal relationship'.

YOUTH: Horizontal relationship?

PHILOSOPHER: Let's start with an easily understood example, that of the parent–child relationship. Whether the circumstances are those of childrearing, or of training junior staff in the workplace, for example, generally speaking there are two approaches that are considered: one is the method of raising by rebuke, and the other is the method of raising by praise.

YOUTH: Ah. That is a hotly debated issue.

PHILOSOPHER: Which one do you think is the better choice? To rebuke or to praise?

YOUTH: It's better to raise by praising, of course.

PHILOSOPHER: Why?

YOUTH: Take animal training, for example. When teaching animals to do tricks, you can make them obey with a whip. This is the typical 'raising by rebuke' way. On the other hand, it's also possible to get animals to learn tricks by holding up rewards of food or saying kind words. This is 'raising by praise'. Both ways can lead to the same results—they learn new tricks. But the motivation for moving toward the objective is completely different if the animal is doing it because it will be rebuked or doing it because it wants to be praised. In the latter instance, it will come with a feeling of joy. Rebuke only makes the animal wither. But raising with praise naturally allows it to grow strong and healthy. This seems like an obvious conclusion.

PHILOSOPHER: Animal training is an interesting example. Now, let's look at this from the standpoint of Adlerian psychology. In Adlerian psychology, we take the stance that in childrearing, and in all other forms of communication with other people, one must not praise.

YOUTH: One must not praise?

PHILOSOPHER: Physical punishment is out of the question, of course, and rebuking is not accepted, either. One must not praise, and one must not rebuke. That is the standpoint of Adlerian psychology.

YOUTH: But how is that even possible?

PHILOSOPHER: Consider the reality of the act of praise. For example, suppose I praised a statement you made by saying, 'Good job!' Wouldn't hearing those words seem strange somehow?

YOUTH: Yes, I guess it would put me in an unpleasant mood.

PHILOSOPHER: Can you explain why it would feel unpleasant?

YOUTH: What's unpleasant is the feeling that from the words 'Good job!' one is being talked down to.

PHILOSOPHER: Exactly. In the act of praise, there is the aspect of it being 'the passing of judgement by a person of ability on a person of no ability'. A mother praises her child who has helped her prepare dinner, saying, 'You're such a good helper!' But when her husband does the same things, you can be sure she won't be telling him, 'You're such a good helper!'

YOUTH: Ha-ha, you are right about that.

PHILOSOPHER: In other words, the mother who praises the child by saying things like 'You're such a good helper!' or 'Good job!' or 'Well, aren't you something!' is unconsciously creating a hierarchical relationship and seeing the child as beneath her. The example of animal training that you just gave is also emblematic of the hierarchical relationship—the vertical relationship—that is behind the praising. When one person praises another, the goal is 'to manipulate someone who has less ability than you'. It is not done out of gratitude or respect.

YOUTH: So, you're saying that one praises in order to manipulate?

PHILOSOPHER: That's right. Whether we praise or rebuke others, the only difference is one of the carrot or the stick, and the background goal is manipulation. The reason that Adlerian psychology is highly critical of reward-and-punishment education is that its intention is to manipulate children.

YOUTH: No way, you're wrong there. Because think of it from the standpoint of the child. For children, isn't being praised by their parents the greatest joy of all? It's because they want praise that they do their studies. It's because they want praise that they learn to behave properly. That's how it was for me when I was a child. How I craved praise from my parents! And even after becoming an adult, it's been the same way. When your boss praises you, it feels good. That's how it is for everyone. This has nothing to do with reason—it's just instinctual emotion!

PHILOSOPHER: One wishes to be praised by someone. Or conversely, one decides to give praise to someone. This is proof that one is seeing all interpersonal relationships as 'vertical relationships'. This holds true for you, too: it is because you are living in vertical relationships that you want to be praised. Adlerian psychology refutes all manner of vertical relationships, and proposes that all interpersonal relationships be horizontal relationships. In a sense, this point may be regarded as the fundamental principle of Adlerian psychology.

YOUTH: Is this something that is conveyed by the words 'equal but not the same'?

PHILOSOPHER: Yes. Equal, that is to say, horizontal. For example, there are men who verbally abuse their wives, who do all the house-work, with such remarks as, 'You're not bringing in any money, so I don't want to hear it' or 'It's thanks to me that there's food on the table.' And I'm sure you've heard this one before: 'You have everything you need, so what are you complaining about?' It's perfectly shameful. Such statements of economic superiority or the like have no connection whatsoever to human worth. A company employee and a full-time housewife simply have different workplaces and roles, and are truly 'equal but not the same'.

YOUTH: I agree entirely.

PHILOSOPHER: They are probably afraid that women will grow wise to their situation and start earning more than men do, and that women will start asserting themselves. They see all interpersonal relations as vertical relationships, and they are afraid of being seen by women as beneath them. That is to say, they have intense, hidden feelings of inferiority.

YOUTH: So, in a sense, they are getting into a superiority complex in which they are trying to make a show of their abilities?

PHILOSOPHER: So it seems. In the first place, the feeling of inferiority is an awareness that arises within vertical relationships. If one can build horizontal relationships that are 'equal but not the same' for all people, there will no longer be any room for inferiority complexes to emerge.

YOUTH: Hmm. Maybe I do have an awareness of manipulation somewhere in my psyche when I go about praising other people. Laying on the flattery to get in good favour with my boss—that's definitely manipulation, isn't it? And it's the other way around, too. I've been manipulated by being praised by others. Funny, I guess that's just the sort of person I am!

PHILOSOPHER: Yes; in the sense that you have not been able to break out of vertical relationships, it would seem so.

YOUTH: This is getting interesting! Please go on!

THE ENCOURAGEMENT APPROACH

PHILOSOPHER: As you may recall from our discussion on the separation of tasks, I brought up the subject of intervention. This is the act of intruding on other people's tasks. So, why does a person intervene? Here, too, in the background, vertical relationships are at play. It is precisely because one perceives interpersonal relations as vertical, and sees the other party as beneath one, that one intervenes. Through intervention, one tries to lead the other party in the desired direction. One has convinced oneself that one is right, and that the other party is wrong. Of course, the intervention here is manipulation, pure and simple. Parents commanding a child to study is a typical example of this. They might be acting out of the best of intentions from their points of view, but, when it comes down to it, the parents are intruding, and attempting to manipulate the child to go in their desired direction.

YOUTH: If one can build horizontal relationships, will that intervention disappear?

PHILOSOPHER: Yes, it will.

YOUTH: Well, it's one thing if you're just talking about a child's studies. But when someone's suffering right there in front of you, you can't just leave them be, can you? Would you still say that lending a helping hand is intervention, and then do nothing?

PHILOSOPHER: One must not let it go unnoticed. It is necessary to offer assistance that does not turn into intervention.

YOUTH: What is the difference between intervention and assistance?

PHILOSOPHER: Think back to our discussion of the separation of tasks; to the subject of a child's schoolwork. As I stated then, this is a task that the child has to resolve himself, not something that parents or teachers can do for him. So, intervention is this kind of intruding on other people's tasks, and directing them by saying things like, 'You have to study,' or 'Get into that university.' Whereas, assistance, on the other hand, presupposes the separation of tasks, and also horizontal relationships. Having understood that studying is the child's task, one considers what one can do for him. Concretely speaking, instead of commanding from above that the child must study, one acts on him in such a way that he can gain the confidence to take care of his own studies and face his tasks on his own.

YOUTH: And that action isn't forced?

PHILOSOPHER: No, it's not. Without forcing, and with the tasks always kept separate, one assists the child to resolve them by his own efforts. It's the approach of 'you can lead a horse to water, but you can't make him drink'. He is the one who has to face his tasks, and he is the one who makes the resolution.

YOUTH: So, you neither praise nor rebuke?

PHILOSOPHER: That's right, one neither praises nor rebukes. This kind of assistance, which is based on horizontal relationships, is referred to in Adlerian psychology as 'encouragement'.

YOUTH: Encouragement, huh? Right, that's the term you mentioned some time ago. You said you'd explain at a later date.

PHILOSOPHER: When one is not following through with one's tasks, it is not because one is without ability. Adlerian psychology tells us that the issue here is not one of ability, but simply that 'one has lost the *courage* to face one's tasks'. And, if that is the case, the thing to do before anything else is to recover that lost courage.

YOUTH: But, but we're just going around in circles! That's basically the same as giving praise. When one is praised by another person, one becomes truly aware of one's ability and regains one's courage. Please do not be stubborn about this point—just acknowledge the necessity of giving praise.

PHILOSOPHER: No, I will not acknowledge that.

YOUTH: Why not?

PHILOSOPHER: The reason is clear. Being praised is what leads people to form the belief that they have no ability.

YOUTH: What did you say?

PHILOSOPHER: Shall I repeat myself? The more one is praised by another person, the more one forms the belief that one has no ability. Please do your best to remember this.

YOUTH: Do such foolish people even exist? It's got to be the other way around! It is as a result of being praised that one becomes truly aware of one's ability. Isn't that obvious?

PHILOSOPHER: You are wrong. Even if you do derive joy from being praised, it is the same as being dependent on vertical relationships, and acknowledging that you have no ability. Because giving praise is a judgement that is passed by a person of ability onto a person without ability.

YOUTH: I just cannot agree with that.

PHILOSOPHER: When receiving praise becomes one's goal, one is choosing a way of living that is in line with another person's system of values. Looking at your life until now, aren't you tired of trying to live up to your parents' expectations?

YOUTH: Um, well, I guess so.

PHILOSOPHER: First, do the separation of tasks. Then, while accepting each other's differences, build equal horizontal relationships. Encouragement is the approach that comes next.

HOW TO FEEL YOU HAVE VALUE

YOUTH: So, concretely speaking, how does one go about this? One cannot praise, and one cannot rebuke. What other words and choices are there?

PHILOSOPHER: Think about a time when you've had help in your work—not from a child, but from a partner who is your equal—and you will probably see the answer right away. When a friend helps you clean your home, what do you say to him?

YOUTH: I say, 'Thank you.'

PHILOSOPHER: Right. You convey words of gratitude, saying thank you to this partner who has helped you with your work. You might express straightforward delight: 'I'm glad.' Or you could convey your thanks by saying, 'That was a big help.' This is an approach to encouragement that is based on horizontal relationships.

YOUTH: That's all?

PHILOSOPHER: Yes. The most important thing is to not judge other people. Judgement is a word that comes out of vertical relationships. If one is building horizontal relationships, there will be words of more straightforward gratitude and respect and joy.

YOUTH: Hmm, your point that judgement is created by vertical relationships certainly seems to be true. But, what about this? Could the words 'thank you' actually have such a great power as to be able to bring back courage? After all, I think I'd prefer to be praised, even if the words I hear are ones that come from vertical relationships.

PHILOSOPHER: Being praised essentially means that one is receiving judgement from another person as 'good'. And the measure of what is good or bad about that act is that person's yardstick. If receiving praise is what one is after, one will have no choice but to adapt to that person's yardstick and put the brakes on one's own freedom. 'Thank you', on the other hand, rather than being judgement, is a clear expression of gratitude. When one hears words of gratitude, one knows that one has made a contribution to another person.

YOUTH: So, even if you're judged as 'good' by another person, you don't feel that you've made a contribution?

PHILOSOPHER: That's right. This is a point that will connect to our subsequent discussion as well—in Adlerian psychology, a great deal of emphasis is given to 'contribution'.

YOUTH: Why is that?

PHILOSOPHER: Well, what does a person have to do to get *courage*? In Adler's view, 'It is only when a person is able to feel that he has worth that he can possess courage.'

YOUTH: When a person is able to feel that he has worth?

PHILOSOPHER: Do you recall when we were discussing the feeling of inferiority, how I spoke of this as being an issue of subjective worth? Is one able to feel one has worth, or does one feel one is a worthless being? If one is able to feel one has worth, then one can accept oneself just as one is and have the courage to face one's life tasks. So, the issue that arises at this point is, how on earth can one become able to feel one has worth?

YOUTH: Yes, that's it exactly! I need you to explain that very clearly, please.

PHILOSOPHER: It's quite simple. It is when one is able to feel *I am beneficial to the community* that one can have a true sense of one's worth. This is the answer that would be offered in Adlerian psychology.

YOUTH: That I am beneficial to the community?

PHILOSOPHER: That one can act on the community; that is to say, on other people, and that one can feel *I am of use to someone.* Instead of feeling judged by another person as 'good', being able to feel, by way of one's own subjective viewpoint, that *I can make contributions to other people.* It is at that point that, at last, we can have a true sense of our own worth. Everything we have been discussing about community feeling and encouragement connects here.

YOUTH: Hmm. I don't know, it's starting to get a bit confusing.

PHILOSOPHER: We are getting to the heart of the discussion now. Please stick with me a while longer. It is about having concern for others, building horizontal relationships and taking the approach of encouragement. All these things connect to the deep life awareness of 'I am of use to someone', and in turn, to your courage to live.

YOUTH: To be of use to someone. That is what my life is worth living for . . . ?

PHILOSOPHER: Let's take a little break. Would you like some coffee?

YOUTH: Yes, please.

The discussion of community feeling had become more confusing than ever. One must not praise. And one must not rebuke, either. All words that are used to judge other people are words that come out of vertical relationships, and we need to build horizontal relationships. And it is only when one is able to feel that one is of use to someone that one can have a true awareness of one's worth. There was a major flaw in this logic somewhere. The young man felt it instinctively. As he sipped the hot coffee, thoughts of his grandfather crossed his mind.

EXIST IN THE PRESENT

PHILOSOPHER: Well, have you worked things out?

YOUTH: Gradually, but yes, it's getting clearer. You don't seem to be aware of it, but just now you said something really over the top. It's a dangerous, rather extreme opinion that just negates everything in the world.

PHILOSOPHER: Oh, really? What is it?

YOUTH: It's the idea that being of use to someone is what gives one a true awareness of one's worth. If you put it the other way around, a person who isn't of any use to others has no worth at all. That's what you are saying, isn't it? If one takes that to its logical conclusion then the lives of newborn babies, and of invalids and old people who are bedridden, aren't worth living either. How could this be? Let's talk about my grandfather. He spends his days bedridden at an old people's home. Since he has dementia, he doesn't recognise any of his children or grandchildren, and his condition is such that he would not be able to go on living without constant care. One simply couldn't think of him as being of use to someone. Don't you see? Your opinion is basically the same thing as saying to my grandfather, 'People like you aren't qualified to live!'

PHILOSOPHER: I reject that definitively.

YOUTH: How do you reject that?

PHILOSOPHER: There are parents who refute my explanation of the concept of encouragement by saying, 'Our child does bad things from morning to night, and there is never an occasion to tell him, "Thank you" or "You helped a lot."' The context is probably the same as what you are talking about, isn't it?

YOUTH: Yes, it is. So, tell me please how you justify that.

PHILOSOPHER: At this point, you are looking at another person on the level of his acts. In other words, that that person 'did something'. So, from that point of view, it might seem that bedridden old people are only a nuisance, and are of no use to anyone. So, let's look at other people not on the 'level of acts', but on the 'level of being'. Without judging whether or not other people did something, one rejoices in their being there, in their very existence, and one calls out to them with words of gratitude.

YOUTH: You call out to their existence? What on earth are you talking about?

PHILOSOPHER: If you consider things at the level of being, we are of use to others and have worth just by being here. This is an indisputable fact.

YOUTH: No way! Enough joking around. Being of use to someone just by being here—that's got to be straight out of some new religion.

PHILOSOPHER: Well, for example, suppose your mother has a car accident. Her condition is serious, and her life may be in danger.

At a time like that, you would not be wondering if your mother 'did something', or anything of the sort. More than likely, you will just be thinking you'll be glad if she makes it, and you're glad she is holding on right now.

YOUTH: Of course I would!

PHILOSOPHER: That's what it means to be grateful on the level of being. Your mother might not be able to do anything in her critical condition that would be considered an act, but just by being alive, she would be supporting the psychological state of you and your family, and would therefore be of use. The same could be said for you, too. If your life were in danger, and you were hanging on by a thread, the people around you would probably feel very gladdened just by the very fact of your existing. They would simply feel thankful that you are safe in the here and now, and would not be wanting you to perform some direct act. At the very least, there is no reason they would have to think that way. So, instead of thinking of oneself on the level of acts, first of all one accepts oneself on the level of being.

YOUTH: That's an extreme example—everyday life is different.

PHILOSOPHER: No, it is the same.

YOUTH: What is the same about it? Try and give me a more everyday example, please. If you can't, I won't be able to agree with this.

PHILOSOPHER: All right. When we look at other people, we are prone to construct our own ideal images of ourselves, which we then detract from and judge. Imagine, for example, a child who never talks back to his parents, excels in both schoolwork and sports, attends a good university, and joins a large company. There are parents who will compare their child to such an image of an ideal child—which is an impossible fiction—and then be filled with complaints and dissatisfaction. They treat the idealised image as one hundred points, and they gradually subtract from that. This is truly a 'judgement' way of thinking. Instead, the parents could refrain from comparing their child to anyone else, see him for who he actually is, and be glad and grateful for his being there. Instead of taking away points from some idealised image, they could start from zero. And if they do that, they should be able to call out to his existence itself.

YOUTH: Okay, but I'd say that's just an idealistic approach. So, are you saying that even with the kind of child who never goes to school or gets a job, but just shuts himself in and stays home, one should still communicate one's gratitude and say 'thank you'?

PHILOSOPHER: Of course. Suppose your shut-in child helped you wash the dishes after a meal. If you were to say then, 'Enough of that already—just go to school,' you would be using the words of such parents who detract from an image of an ideal child. If you were to take such an approach, the child would probably end up even more discouraged. However, if you can say a straightforward 'thank you', the child just might feel his own worth, and take a new step forward.

YOUTH: That's just utterly hypocritical! It's nothing more than the nonsensical talk of a hypocrite. It sounds like the 'neighbourly love' that Christians talk about. The community feeling, the horizontal relationships, the gratitude for existence and so on. Who on earth could actually do such things?

PHILOSOPHER: With regard to this issue of community feeling, there was a person who asked Adler a similar question. Adler's reply was the following: 'Someone has to start. Other people might not be cooperative, but that is not connected to you. My advice is this: you should start. With no regard to whether others are cooperative or not.' My advice is exactly the same.

PEOPLE CANNOT MAKE
PROPER USE OF SELF

YOUTH: I should start?

PHILOSOPHER: That's right. Without regard to whether other people are cooperative or not.

YOUTH: All right, I'll ask you again. 'People can be of use to someone else simply by being alive, and have a true sense of their worth just by being alive.' Is that what you are saying?

PHILOSOPHER: Yes.

YOUTH: Well, I don't know. I am alive, right here and now. 'I', who is no one else but me, am alive right here. But even so, I don't really feel that I have worth.

PHILOSOPHER: Can you describe in words why you do not feel that you have worth?

YOUTH: I suppose it's what you've been referring to as interpersonal relations. From childhood up to the present, I have always been belittled by people around me, especially my parents, as a poor excuse for a little brother. They have never really tried to recognise me for who I am. You say that worth is something one gives to oneself. But that's just an impracticable theory. For example, at the library where I work, for the most part my job is just sorting the returned books and putting them back on the shelves. It's routine work that anyone could do once they've been taught. If I stopped going to work, my boss would have no trouble finding someone to replace me. I am needed only for the unskilled labour I provide, and it doesn't actually matter at all if it is 'I' who is working there or someone else, or a machine for that matter. No one is requiring 'this me' in particular. In such circumstances, would you have confidence in yourself? Would you be able to have a true sense of worth?

PHILOSOPHER: From an Adlerian psychology point of view, the answer is simple. First of all, build a horizontal relationship between yourself and another person. One is enough. Let's start from there.

YOUTH: Please don't treat me like a fool! Look, I have friends. And I am building solid horizontal relationships with them.

PHILOSOPHER: Even so, I suspect that with your parents and your boss, and with your junior colleagues and other people as well, the relationships you are building are vertical ones.

YOUTH: Of course, I have different kinds of relationships. That's how it is for everyone.

PHILOSOPHER: This is a very important point. Does one build vertical relationships, or does one build horizontal relationships? This is an issue of lifestyle, and human beings are not so clever as to be able to have different lifestyles available whenever the need arises. In other words, deciding that one is 'equal to this person' or 'in a hierarchical relationship with that person' does not work.

YOUTH: Do you mean that one has to choose one or the other— vertical relationships or horizontal relationships?

PHILOSOPHER: Absolutely, yes. If you are building even one vertical relationship with someone, before you even notice what is happening, you will be treating all your interpersonal relations as vertical.

YOUTH: So, I am treating even my relationships with my friends as vertical?

PHILOSOPHER: That is correct. Even if you are not treating them in a boss-or-subordinate kind of way, it is as if you are saying, 'A is above me, and B is below me,' for example, or 'I'll follow A's advice, but ignore what B says,' or 'I don't mind breaking my promise to C.'

YOUTH: Hmm!

PHILOSOPHER: On the other hand, if one has managed to build a horizontal relationship with at least one person—if one has been able to build a relationship of equals in the true sense of the term—that is a major lifestyle transformation. With that breakthrough, all one's interpersonal relations will gradually become horizontal.

YOUTH: What nonsense! There are so many ways I could refute that. Think of a company setting, for example. It wouldn't really be feasible for the director and his new recruits to form relationships as equals, would it? Hierarchical relationships are part of the system of our society, and to ignore that is to ignore the social order. Look, if you heard that a new recruit at your company, who's only twenty or so, had suddenly started buddying up to the sixty-something director, don't you think it would sound pretty far-fetched?

PHILOSOPHER: It is certainly important to respect one's elders. In a company structure, it is only natural for there to be different levels of responsibility. I am not telling you to make friends with everyone, or behave as if you are close friends. Rather, what is important is to be equal in consciousness, and to assert that which needs to be asserted.

YOUTH: I am not someone who can mouth off to my seniors, and I would never think of trying. My social commonsense would be called into question if I did.

PHILOSOPHER: What is 'senior'? What is this 'mouthing off'? If one is gauging the atmosphere of a situation and being dependent on vertical relationships, one is engaging in irresponsible acts—one is trying to avoid one's responsibilities.

YOUTH: What is irresponsible about it?

PHILOSOPHER: Suppose that as a result of following your boss's instructions, your work ends in failure. Whose responsibility is it then?

YOUTH: Well, that'd be my boss's responsibility. Because I was just following orders, and he was the one who decided on them.

PHILOSOPHER: None of the responsibility is yours?

YOUTH: No, it isn't. It's the responsibility of the boss who gave the orders. This is what's known as organisational accountability.

PHILOSOPHER: You are wrong. That is a life-lie. There *is* space for you to refuse, and there should also be space to propose a better way of doing things. You are just thinking there is no space to refuse so that you can avoid the conflict of the associated interpersonal relations and avoid responsibility—and you are being dependent on vertical relationships.

YOUTH: Are you saying I should disobey my boss? Sure, in theory, I should. Theoretically, it's exactly as you say. But I can't do that! There's no way I could build a relationship like that.

PHILOSOPHER: Really? You are building a horizontal relationship with me right now. You are asserting yourself very well. Instead of thinking about this or that difficulty, you can just start here.

YOUTH: I can start here?

PHILOSOPHER: Yes, in this small study. As I told you earlier, to me, you are an irreplaceable friend.

YOUTH: ...

PHILOSOPHER: Am I wrong?

YOUTH: I appreciate it, I really do. But I am afraid. I am afraid of accepting your proposal.

PHILOSOPHER: What are you afraid of, exactly?

YOUTH: The tasks of friendship, naturally. I have never befriended an older man like you. I have no idea if a friend relationship with such a difference in age is even possible, or if I had better think of it as a student–teacher relationship.

PHILOSOPHER: Age does not matter in love and friendship. It is certainly true that the tasks of friendship require a steady courage. With regard to your relationship with me, it will be fine to reduce the distance little by little. To a degree of distance in which we are not in very close contact, but can still reach out and touch each other's faces with our outstretched arms, so to speak.

YOUTH: Please give me some time. Just once more, I would like some time to try to figure things out on my own. Our discussion today has given me much to think about. I would like to take it all home and ruminate on it calmly on my own.

PHILOSOPHER: It takes time to gain a true understanding of community feeling. It would be quite impossible to understand everything about it right here and now. Please return to your home and give it some careful thought, while checking it against everything else we have discussed.

YOUTH: I will. In any case, it was quite a blow to be told that I never really look at others, and I only have concern for myself. You're really a dreadful fellow!

PHILOSOPHER: Ha-ha. You say it in such a happy way.

YOUTH: Yes, I enjoy it immensely. It hurts, of course. It's like a sharp pain that shoots through me, as if I were swallowing needles. But still, I enjoy it immensely. It's habit-forming, having these discussions with you. I realised a little while ago that maybe I don't just want to take apart your argument—I want you to take apart mine, too.

PHILOSOPHER: I see. That's an interesting analysis.

YOUTH: But don't forget. I told you that I am going to take apart your argument and bring you to your knees, and I haven't given up.

PHILOSOPHER: Thank you. I've had a good time, too. Come by whenever you're ready to pick this back up.

THE
FIFTH
NIGHT

*To live in earnest in
the here and now*

The young man thought to himself: *Adlerian psychology is engaged in a thorough inquiry into interpersonal relationships. And the final goal of these interpersonal relationships is community feeling. But is this really enough? Isn't there something else that I was brought into this world to achieve? What is the meaning of life? Where am I headed, and what sort of life am I trying to lead?* The more the young man thought, the more it seemed to him that his own existence had been tiny and insignificant.

EXCESSIVE SELF-CONSCIOUSNESS STIFLES THE SELF

PHILOSOPHER: It's been a while, hasn't it?

YOUTH: Yes, I last came about a month ago. I have been thinking about the meaning of community feeling since then.

PHILOSOPHER: So, how do you feel about it now?

YOUTH: Well, community feeling is definitely an attractive idea. The sense of belonging, that 'it's okay to be here', for example, which we possess as a fundamental desire. I think it is a brilliant insight into our existence as social creatures.

PHILOSOPHER: It's a brilliant insight, except . . . ?

YOUTH: Funny, you caught on right away. That's right, I still have some issues with it. I'll say it straight out—I have no idea what you are going on about with your references to the universe and all that, and it ends up reeking of religion from beginning to end. There's this kind of cultish quality to it all that I just can't shake.

PHILOSOPHER: When Adler first proposed the concept of community feeling, there was a great deal of opposition in a similar vein. People said that psychology is supposed to be a science, and here was Adler discussing the issue of worth. That sort of thing isn't science, they said.

YOUTH: So, in my own way, I tried to figure out why I couldn't understand what you were talking about, and I'm thinking that the order of things might be the problem. You're starting off with the universe and inanimate objects, and the past and the future and so on, so I lose track of things. Instead, one should get a firm grasp of the 'I'. Next, one should contemplate one-on-one relationships. That is to say, the interpersonal relationships of 'you and I'. And once one has done that, the larger community should come into view.

PHILOSOPHER: I see. That is a good order.

YOUTH: Now, the first thing I want to ask about is attachment to self. You are saying that one has to stop being attached to the 'I' and make the switch to 'concern for others'. I am sure it is exactly as you say—concern for others is important, I agree. But no matter what, we worry about ourselves; we look at ourselves all the time.

PHILOSOPHER: Have you thought about why we worry about ourselves?

YOUTH: I have. If I were a narcissist, for example—if I were in love with myself and constantly fascinated with myself—maybe that would simplify things. Because your instruction, 'have more concern for others', is a perfectly sound one. But I am not a self-loving narcissist. I am a self-loathing realist. I hate who I am, and that's exactly why I look at myself all the time. I don't have confidence in myself, and that's why I am excessively self-conscious.

PHILOSOPHER: At what times do you feel that you are excessively self-conscious?

YOUTH: Well, at meetings for example, I have a hard time raising my hand and making myself heard. I think needless things, like *If I ask this question, they'll probably laugh at me* or *If the point I want to make is irrelevant, I'll get ridiculed,* and so on, and I just clam up. Truthfully, I falter even when it comes to telling silly jokes in front of people. Every time, my self-consciousness kicks in and puts the brakes on, and it's as if I've been straightjacketed. My self-consciousness won't allow me to behave in an innocent way. But I don't even have to ask for your answer. I'm sure it'll be the same as always: have courage. But you know, such words are of no use to me. Because this isn't just a matter of courage.

PHILOSOPHER: I see. Last time, I gave an overview of community feeling. Today, we will dig deeper.

YOUTH: And where will that take us?

PHILOSOPHER: We will probably arrive at the question, what is happiness?

YOUTH: Oh! So, happiness lies beyond community feeling?

PHILOSOPHER: There is no need to rush the answers. What we need is dialogue.

YOUTH: All right, then. So, let's get started!

NOT SELF-AFFIRMATION—
SELF-ACCEPTANCE

PHILOSOPHER: First of all, let's look at what you were just saying, about your self-consciousness putting the brakes on and not letting you behave in an innocent way. There are probably many people who experience this trouble. So, let's go back to the source again, and think about your goal. What could you be trying to gain by putting the brakes on your own innocent behaviour?

YOUTH: It's the genuine desire to not be laughed at; to not be thought of as a fool.

PHILOSOPHER: So, in other words, you do not have confidence in your innocent self; in yourself just as you are, right? And you stay away from the kind of interpersonal relationship in which you would just be yourself. But I'll bet that when you're home alone, you sing out loud and dance to music, and speak in a lively voice.

YOUTH: Ha-ha! It's almost like you've set up a surveillance camera in my room! But yes, it's true. I can behave freely when I'm alone.

PHILOSOPHER: Anyone can behave like a king when they're alone. So, this is an issue that should be considered in the context of inter-personal relations. Because it isn't that you don't have an innocent self—it is only that you can't do such things in front of others.

YOUTH: Well, what should I do then?

PHILOSOPHER: It's about community feeling, after all. Concretely speaking, it's making the switch from attachment to self (self-interest) to concern for others (social interest), and gaining a sense of community feeling. Three things are needed at this point: 'self-acceptance', 'confidence in others' and 'contribution to others'.

YOUTH: Interesting. New keywords, I see. What do they refer to?

PHILOSOPHER: Let's start with self-acceptance. On our first night, I brought up that statement of Adler's: 'The important thing is not what one is born with, but what use one makes of that equipment.' Do you remember this?

YOUTH: Yes, of course.

PHILOSOPHER: We cannot discard the receptacle that is the 'I', and neither can we replace it. The important thing, however, is 'what use one makes of that equipment'. One changes one's way of looking at the 'I'— that is to say, one changes how one uses it.

YOUTH: Does that mean be more positive and have a stronger sense of self-affirmation? Think about everything more positively?

PHILOSOPHER: There is no need to go out of one's way to be positive and affirm oneself. It's not self-affirmation that we are concerned with, but self-acceptance.

YOUTH: Not self-affirmation, but self-acceptance?

PHILOSOPHER: That's right. There is a clear difference. Self-affirmation is making suggestions to oneself, such as 'I can do it' or

'I am strong', even when something is simply beyond one's ability. It is a notion that can bring about a superiority complex, and may even be termed a way of living in which one lies to oneself. With self-acceptance, on the other hand, if one cannot do something, one is simply accepting 'one's incapable self' as is, and moving forward so that one can do whatever one can. It is not a way of lying to oneself. To put it more simply, say you've got a score of sixty per cent, but you tell yourself *I just happened to get unlucky this time around, and the real me is one hundred per cent.* That is self-affirmation. By contrast, if one accepts oneself as one is, as sixty per cent, and thinks to oneself, *How should I go about getting closer to one hundred per cent?*—that is self-acceptance.

YOUTH: So, even if you're only sixty per cent, there's no need to be pessimistic?

PHILOSOPHER: Of course not. No one is perfect. Do you recall what I said when I was explaining the pursuit of superiority? That all people are in this condition of wanting to improve? Put the other way around, there is no such thing as a one hundred per cent person. This is something we should actively acknowledge.

YOUTH: Hmm. What you are saying sounds positive in various respects, but has a negative ring to it as well.

PHILOSOPHER: Here, I use the term 'affirmative resignation'.

YOUTH: Affirmative resignation?

PHILOSOPHER: This is also the case with the separation of tasks—one ascertains the things one can change and the things one cannot change. One cannot change what one is born with. But one can, under one's own power, go about changing what use one makes of that equipment. So, in that case, one simply has to focus on what one can change, rather than on what one cannot. This is what I call self-acceptance.

YOUTH: What one can change, and what one cannot.

PHILOSOPHER: That's right. Accept what is irreplaceable. Accept 'this me' just as it is. And have the *courage* to change what one can change. That is self-acceptance.

YOUTH: Hmm. That reminds me of a line that the writer Kurt Vonnegut quoted in one of his books: 'God grant me the serenity to accept the things I cannot change, courage to change the things I can, and wisdom always to tell the difference.' It's in the novel *Slaughterhouse-Five*.

PHILOSOPHER: Yes, I know it. It is the Serenity Prayer. These words are well known, and have been transmitted for many years in Christian societies.

YOUTH: He even used the word *courage*. I read the book so intently I should know it by heart. But I never noticed this point until now.

PHILOSOPHER: It's true. We do not lack ability. We just lack *courage*. It all comes down to *courage*.

THE DIFFERENCE BETWEEN
TRUST AND CONFIDENCE

YOUTH: There is something about this 'affirmative resignation' that sounds pessimistic. It's just too bleak if the upshot of all this lengthy discussion is resignation.

PHILOSOPHER: Is that so? Resignation has the connotation of seeing clearly with fortitude and acceptance. Having a firm grasp on the truth of things—that is resignation. There is nothing pessimistic about it.

YOUTH: A firm grasp on the truth . . .

PHILOSOPHER: Of course, just because one has arrived at affirmative resignation as one's self-acceptance, it does not automatically follow that one finds community feeling. That is the reality. When one is switching from attachment to self to concern for others, the second key concept—confidence in others—becomes absolutely essential.

YOUTH: Confidence in others. In other words, *believing* in others?

PHILOSOPHER: Here, I will consider the words 'believing in others' in the context of distinguishing trust from confidence. First, when we speak of trust, we are referring to something that comes with set conditions. In English, it is referred to as credit. For example, when one wants to borrow money from a bank, one has to have some kind of security. The bank calculates the amount of the loan based on the value of that security, and says, 'We will lend you this much.' The attitude of 'we will lend it to you on the condition that you will pay it back,' or 'we will lend you as much as you are able to pay back,' is not one of having confidence in someone. It is trust.

YOUTH: Well, that's how bank financing works, I guess.

PHILOSOPHER: By contrast, from the standpoint of Adlerian psychology, the basis of interpersonal relations is not founded on trust but on confidence.

YOUTH: And 'confidence' in this case is . . . ?

PHILOSOPHER: It is doing without any set conditions whatsoever when believing in others. Even if one does not have sufficient objective grounds for trusting someone, one believes. One believes unconditionally without concerning oneself with such things as security. That is confidence.

YOUTH: Believing unconditionally? So, it's back to your pet notion of neighbourly love?

PHILOSOPHER: Of course, if one believes in others without setting any conditions whatsoever, there will be times when one gets taken advantage of. Just like the guarantor of a debt, there are times when one may suffer damages. The attitude of continuing to believe in someone even in such instances is what we call confidence.

YOUTH: Only a naïve dimwit would do such a thing! I guess you hold with the doctrine of innate human goodness, while I hold with the doctrine of innate human evilness. Believe unconditionally in complete strangers, and you'll just get used and abused.

PHILOSOPHER: And there are also times when someone deceives you, and you get used that way. But look at it from the standpoint of someone who has been taken advantage of. There are people who will continue to believe in you unconditionally even if you are the one who has taken advantage of them. People who will have confidence in you no matter how they are treated. Would you be able to betray such a person again and again?

YOUTH: Um, no. Well, it would be . . .

PHILOSOPHER: I am sure it would be quite difficult for you to do such a thing.

YOUTH: After all that, are you saying one has to appeal to the emotions? To keep on holding the faith, like a saint, and act on the conscience of the other person? You're telling me that morals don't matter to Adler, but isn't that exactly what we're talking about here?

PHILOSOPHER: No, it is not. What would you say is the opposite of confidence?

YOUTH: An antonym of confidence? Uh . . .

PHILOSOPHER: It is doubt. Suppose you have placed 'doubt' at the foundation of your interpersonal relations. That you live your life doubting other people—doubting your friends, and even your family and those you love. What sort of relationship could possibly arise from that? The other person will detect the doubt in your eyes in an instant. He or she will have an instinctive understanding that 'this person does not have confidence in me'. Do you think one would be able to build some kind of positive relationship from that point? It is precisely because we lay a foundation of unconditional confidence that it is possible for us to build a deep relationship.

YOUTH: Okay, I guess.

PHILOSOPHER: The way to understand Adlerian psychology is simple. Right now, you are thinking, *If I were to have confidence in someone unconditionally, I would just get taken advantage of.* However, you are not the one who decides whether or not to take advantage. That is the other person's task. All you need to do is think, *What should I do?* If you are telling yourself, *I'll give it to him if he isn't going take advantage of me,* it is just a relationship of trust that is based on security or conditions.

YOUTH: So, one separates tasks there, too?

PHILOSOPHER: Yes. As I have stated repeatedly, carrying out the separation of tasks returns life to an astonishingly simple form. But while the principle of the separation of tasks is easy to grasp, putting it into practice is difficult. I recognise that.

YOUTH: Then, you are telling me to keep on having confidence in everyone; to keep on believing in all other people even when they deceive me, and just go on being a naïve fool? That's not philosophy or psychology or anything of the sort—it's just the preaching of a zealot!

PHILOSOPHER: I reject that definitively. Adlerian psychology is not saying 'have confidence in others unconditionally' on the basis of a moralistic system of values. Unconditional confidence is a means for making your interpersonal relationship with a person better, and for building a horizontal relationship. If you do not have the desire to make your relationship with that person better, then go ahead and sever it. Because carrying out the severing is your task.

YOUTH: Then, what if I've placed unconditional confidence in a friend in order to make our relationship better? I've jumped through all sorts of hoops for this friend, gladly satisfied any requests for money, and been unstinting with my time and efforts in his regard. But even in such cases, there are times when one is taken advantage of. For example, if one were horribly taken advantage of by a person one has believed in completely, wouldn't that experience lead one to a lifestyle with an 'other people are my enemies' outlook?

PHILOSOPHER: It seems that you have not yet gained an understanding of the goal of confidence. Suppose, for example, that you are in a love relationship, but you are having doubts about your partner and you think to yourself, *I'll bet she's cheating on me.* And you start making desperate efforts in search of evidence to prove that. What do you think would happen as a result?

YOUTH: Well, I guess that would depend on the situation.

PHILOSOPHER: No, in every instance, you would find an abundance of evidence that she has been cheating on you.

YOUTH: Wait? Why is that?

PHILOSOPHER: Your partner's casual remarks, her tone when talking to someone on the phone, the times when you can't reach her . . . As long as you are looking with doubt in your eyes, everything around you will appear to be evidence that she is cheating on you. Even if she is not.

YOUTH: Hmm.

PHILOSOPHER: Right now, you are only concerned about the times you were taken advantage of, and nothing else. You focus only on the pain from the wounds you sustained on such occasions. But if you are afraid to have confidence in others, in the long run, you will not be able to build deep relationships with anyone.

YOUTH: Well, I see what you're getting at—the main objective, which is to build deep relationships. But still, being taken advantage of is scary, and that's the reality, isn't it?

PHILOSOPHER: If it is a shallow relationship, when it falls apart the pain will be slight. And the joy that relationship brings each day will also be slight. It is precisely because one can gain the courage to enter into deeper relationships by having confidence in others that the joy of one's interpersonal relations can grow, and one's joy in life can grow, too.

YOUTH: No! That's not what I was talking about, you're changing the subject again. The courage to overcome the fear of being taken advantage of—where does it come from?

PHILOSOPHER: It comes from self-acceptance. If one can simply accept oneself as one is, and ascertain what one can do and what one cannot, one becomes able to understand that 'taking advantage' is the other person's task, and getting to the core of 'confidence in others' becomes less difficult.

YOUTH: You're saying that taking advantage of someone is the other person's task, and one can't do anything about it? That I should be resigned, in an affirmative way? Your arguments always ignore our emotions. What does one do about all the anger and sadness one feels when one is taken advantage of?

PHILOSOPHER: When one is sad, one should be sad to one's heart's content. It is precisely when one tries to escape the pain and sadness that one gets stuck and ceases to be able to build deep relationships with anyone. Think about it this way. We can believe. And we can doubt. But we are aspiring to see others as our comrades. To believe or to doubt—the choice should be clear.

THE ESSENCE OF WORK
IS A CONTRIBUTION TO
THE COMMON GOOD

YOUTH: All right. Well, suppose I have managed to attain self-acceptance. And that I have attained confidence in others, too. What kind of changes would there be in me, then?

PHILOSOPHER: First, one accepts one's irreplaceable 'this me' just as it is. That is self-acceptance. Then, one places unconditional confidence in other people. That is confidence in others. You can accept yourself, and you can have confidence in others. So, what are other people to you now?

YOUTH: ... My comrades?

PHILOSOPHER: Exactly. In effect, placing confidence in others is connected to seeing others as comrades. It is because they are one's comrades that one can have confidence in them. If they were not one's comrades, one would not be able to reach the level of confidence. And then, having other people as one's comrades connects to finding refuge in the community one belongs to. So, one can gain the sense of belonging that 'it's okay to be here'.

YOUTH: In other words, you're saying that to feel 'it's okay to be here' one has to see others as comrades. And that to see others as comrades, one needs both self-acceptance and confidence in others.

PHILOSOPHER: That's right. You are grasping this more quickly now. To take it a step farther, one may say that people who think of others as enemies have not attained self-acceptance, and do not have enough confidence in others.

YOUTH: All right. It is true that people seek the sense of belonging that 'it's okay to be here'. And, to get that, they need self-acceptance and confidence in others. I have no objection to that. But, I don't know. Can one really gain a sense of belonging just by seeing others as comrades, and having confidence in them?

PHILOSOPHER: Of course, community feeling is not something that is attainable with just self-acceptance and confidence in others. It is at this point that the third key concept—contribution to others—becomes necessary.

YOUTH: Contribution to others?

PHILOSOPHER: Is to act, in some way, on one's comrades. To attempt to contribute. That is 'contribution to others'.

YOUTH: So, when you say 'contribute', you mean to show a spirit of self-sacrifice and to be of service to those around you?

PHILOSOPHER: Contribution to others does not connote self-sacrifice. Adler goes so far as to warn that those who sacrifice their own lives for others are people who have conformed to society too much. And please do not forget: we are truly aware of our own worth only when we feel that our existence and behaviour are beneficial to the community, that is to say, when one feels, 'I am of use to someone.' Do you remember this? In other words, contribution to others, rather than being about getting rid of the 'I' and being of service to someone, is actually something one does in order to be truly aware of the worth of the 'I'.

YOUTH: Contributing to others is for oneself?

PHILOSOPHER: Yes. There is no need to sacrifice the self.

YOUTH: Uh-oh, your argument is starting to crumble here, isn't it? You've done a wonderful job of digging your own grave. In order to satisfy the 'I', one makes oneself of service to others. Isn't that the very definition of hypocrisy? I said it before: your entire argument is hypocritical. It's a slippery argument. Look, I would rather believe in the villain who is honest about his desires, than the good guy who tells a pack of lies.

PHILOSOPHER: Those are a lot of hasty conclusions. You do not understand community feeling yet.

YOUTH: Then I wish you would provide concrete examples of what you consider to be contribution to others.

PHILOSOPHER: The most easily understood contribution to others is probably work. To be in society and join the workforce. Or to do the work of taking care of one's household. Labour is not a means of earning money. It is through labour that one makes contributions to others and commits to one's community, and that one truly feels 'I am of use to someone' and even comes to accept one's existential worth.

YOUTH: You are saying that the essence of work is contribution to others?

PHILOSOPHER: Making money is a major factor too, of course. It is something akin to that Dostoevsky quote you happened upon —'Money is coined freedom.' But there are people who have so much money that they could never use it all. And many of these people are continually busy with their work. Why do they work? Are they driven by boundless greed? No. They work so they are able to contribute to others, and also to confirm their sense of belonging, their feeling that 'it's okay to be here'. Wealthy people who, on having amassed a great fortune, focus their energies on charitable activities, are doing so in order to attain a sense of their own worth and confirm for themselves that 'it's okay to be here'.

YOUTH: Hmm, I suppose that is one truth. But . . .

PHILOSOPHER: But what?

Self-acceptance: accepting one's irreplaceable 'this me' just as it is. Confidence in others: to place unconditional confidence at the base of one's interpersonal relations, rather than seeding doubt. The young man found these two concepts sufficiently convincing. Contribution to others, however, was something he could not quite grasp. *If that contribution is supposed to be 'for other people', then it would have to be one of bitter self-sacrifice. On the other hand, if that contribution is actually 'for oneself', then it's the height of hypocrisy. This point has to be made utterly clear.* In a resolute tone of voice, the young man continued.

YOUNG PEOPLE WALK
AHEAD OF ADULTS

YOUTH: I will acknowledge that work has aspects of contribution to others. But the logic that says that officially one is contributing to others, when, in actuality, one is doing it for oneself, is nothing other than hypocrisy. How do you explain that?

PHILOSOPHER: Imagine the following kind of scene. It's after dinner at home, and there are still dishes left on the table. The children have gone off to their rooms, and the husband is sitting on the sofa watching television. It's been left to the wife (me) to do the dishes and clear everything up. To make matters worse, the family takes that for granted, and they don't make the slightest effort to help. In such a situation, normally one would think, *Why won't they give me a hand?* or *Why do I have to do all the work?* Even if I do not hear the words 'thank you' from my family while I am cleaning up, I want them to think that I am of use to the family. Instead of thinking about what others can do for me, I want to think about, and put into practice, what I can do for other people. Just by having that feeling of contribution, the reality right in front of me will take on a completely different hue. In fact, if I am grumbling to myself as I wash the dishes, I am probably not much fun to be around, so everyone just wants to keep their distance. On the other hand, if I'm humming away to myself and washing the dishes in good spirits, the children might come and give me a hand. At the very least, I'd be creating an atmosphere in which it is easier for them to offer their help.

YOUTH: Well, that might be the case in that setting, anyway.

PHILOSOPHER: Now, how come I have a feeling of contribution in that setting? I have it because I am able to think of the members of my family as comrades. If I cannot do that, inevitably there will be thoughts running through my head like, *Why am I the only one doing this?* and *Why won't anyone give me a hand?* Contribution that is carried out while one is seeing other people as enemies may indeed lead to hypocrisy. But if other people are one's comrades that should never happen, regardless of the contributions one makes. You have been fixating on the word hypocrisy because you do not understand community feeling yet.

YOUTH: Okay . . .

PHILOSOPHER: For the sake of convenience, up to this point I have discussed self-acceptance, confidence in others and contribution to others, in that order. However, these three are linked as an indispensable whole, in a sort of circular structure. It is because one accepts oneself just as one is—one self-accepts—that one can have 'confidence in others' without the fear of being taken advantage of. And it is because one can place unconditional confidence in others, and feel that people are one's comrades, that one can engage in 'contribution to others'. Further, it is because one contributes to others that one can have the deep awareness that 'I am of use to someone,' and accept oneself just as one is. One can self-accept. The notes you took down the other day, do you have them with you?

YOUTH: Oh, you mean that note on the objectives put forward by Adlerian psychology? I've kept it on me ever since that day, of course. Here it is: 'The two objectives for behaviour: to be self-reliant and to live in harmony with society. The two objectives for the psychology that supports these behaviours: the consciousness that *I have the ability* and the consciousness that *people are my comrades*.'

PHILOSOPHER: If you overlap the content of this note with what we have just been discussing, you should be able to gain a deeper understanding. In other words, 'to be self-reliant' and 'the consciousness that *I have the ability*' corresponds to our discussion of self-acceptance. And then 'to live in harmony with society' and 'the consciousness that *people are my comrades*' connects to confidence in others, and then to contribution to others.

YOUTH: I see. So, the objective of life is community feeling. I think it will be some time before I can get this clear in my head, though.

PHILOSOPHER: Yes, it probably will. As Adler himself said, 'Understanding a human being is no easy matter. Of all the forms of psychology, individual psychology is probably the most difficult to learn and put into practice.'

YOUTH: That's exactly right! Even if the theories are convincing, it's hard to put them into practice.

PHILOSOPHER: It is even said that to truly understand Adlerian psychology and apply it to actually changing one's way of living, one needs 'half the number of years one has lived'. In other words, if you were to start studying it at the age of forty, it would take another twenty years, until you turned sixty. If you were to start studying at the age of twenty, it would take ten years, until you turned thirty. You are still young. Starting at such an early stage in life means that you might be able to change more quickly. In the sense that you can change quickly, you are walking ahead of the adults of the world. To go about changing yourself and making a new world, in a way, you are ahead of me, too. It is okay to lose your way or lose focus. Do not be dependent on vertical relationships or be afraid of being disliked, and just make your way forward freely. If all the adults could see that young people were walking ahead of them, I am sure the world would change dramatically.

YOUTH: I am walking ahead of you?

PHILOSOPHER: You certainly are. We walk on the same ground, and you are moving on ahead of me.

YOUTH: Ha-ha. You're the first person I've ever met who would say such a thing to someone young enough to be his son.

PHILOSOPHER: I would like more and more young people to learn about Adler's thought. And I would like more adults to learn about it, too. Because people can change, regardless of their ages.

WORKAHOLISM IS A LIFE-LIE

YOUTH: All right. I readily admit that I do not have the *courage* to take steps toward self-acceptance or confidence in others. But is this really only the fault of the 'I'? Isn't it also actually a problem brought about by other people, who accuse me unreasonably and attack me?

PHILOSOPHER: To be sure, not everyone in the world is a good and virtuous person. One goes through any number of unpleasant experiences in one's interpersonal relations. But there is something one must not get wrong at this juncture: the fact that, in every instance, it is 'that person' who attacks you who has the problem, and it is certainly not the case that everyone is bad. People with neurotic lifestyles tend to sprinkle their speech with such words as 'everyone' and 'always' and 'everything'. 'Everyone hates me,' they will say, or 'It's always me who takes a loss,' or 'Everything is wrong.' If you think you might be in the habit of using such generalising statements, you should be careful.

YOUTH: Well, that does sound rather familiar.

PHILOSOPHER: In Adlerian psychology, we think of this as a way of living that is lacking in 'harmony of life'. It is a way of living in which one sees only a part of things, but judges the whole.

YOUTH: Harmony of life?

PHILOSOPHER: In the teachings of Judaism, one finds the following anecdote: 'If there are ten people, one will be someone who criticises you no matter what you do. This person will come to dislike you, and you will not learn to like him either. Then, there will be two others who accept everything about you and whom you accept too, and you will become close friends with them. The remaining seven people will be neither of these types.' Now, do you focus on the one person who dislikes you? Do you pay more attention to the two who love you? Or would you focus on the crowd, the other seven? A person who is lacking in harmony of life will see only the one person he dislikes, and will make a judgement of the world from that.

YOUTH: Intriguing.

PHILOSOPHER: Some time ago, I participated in a workshop for stammer sufferers and their families. Do you know anyone who has a stammer?

YOUTH: Yes, there was a student at the school I went to who stuttered. That must be hard to deal with, both for the person who has it, and for his family, too.

PHILOSOPHER: Why is stammering hard to deal with? The view in Adlerian psychology is that people who suffer from stammering are concerned only about their own way of speaking, and they have feelings of inferiority and see their lives as unbearably hard. And they become too self-conscious as a result, and start tripping over their words more and more.

YOUTH: They are concerned only about their own way of speaking?

PHILOSOPHER: That's right. There are not many people who will laugh at or make fun of someone when he trips over his words now and then. To use the example I just mentioned, it would probably be no more than one person in ten, at most. In any case, with the sort of foolish person who would take such an attitude, it is best to simply sever the relationship. But if one is lacking in harmony of life, one will focus only on that person and end up thinking, *Everyone is laughing at me.*

YOUTH: But that's just human nature!

PHILOSOPHER: I have a reading group that meets on a regular basis, and one of the participants has a stammer. It comes out sometimes when it's his turn to read. But not a single person there is the sort who would laugh at him for that. Everyone just sits quietly, and waits in a quite natural way for the next words to come out. I am sure this is not a phenomenon that is isolated to my reading group. When one's interpersonal relations do not go well, it cannot be blamed on a stammer or a fear of blushing, or anything of the sort. Even though the problem is really that one has not attained self-acceptance or confidence in others, or contribution to others for that matter, one is focusing on only one tiny part of things that simply should not matter, and from that trying to form judgements with regard to the entire world. This is a misguided lifestyle that is lacking in harmony of life.

YOUTH: Did you actually convey such a harsh idea to people who suffer from stammering?

PHILOSOPHER: Of course. At first, there were some adverse reactions, but by the end of the three-day workshop, everyone was in deep agreement with it.

YOUTH: It certainly is a fascinating argument. But focusing on people who suffer from stammering seems like a rather special example. Could you give me any others?

PHILOSOPHER: Well, another would be the workaholic. This, too, is an example of a person who is clearly lacking in harmony of life.

YOUTH: A workaholic is? Why is that?

PHILOSOPHER: People who suffer from stammering are looking at only a part of things, but judging the whole. With workaholics, the focus is solely on one specific aspect of life.

They probably try to justify that by saying, 'It's busy at work, so I don't have enough time to think about my family.' But this is a life-lie. They are simply trying to avoid their other responsibilities by using work as an excuse. One ought to concern oneself with everything, from household chores and childrearing, to one's friendships and hobbies and so on; Adler does not recognise ways of living in which certain aspects are unusually dominant.

YOUTH: Ah . . . That's exactly the sort of person my father was. It was just: be a workaholic, bury yourself in your work and produce results. And then, rule over the family on the grounds that you are the breadwinner. He was a very feudalistic person.

PHILOSOPHER: In a sense, that is a way of living of refusing to acknowledge one's life tasks. 'Work' does not mean having a job at a company. Work in the home, childrearing, contributing to the local society, hobbies and all manner of other things are work. Companies and such are just one small part of that. A way of living that acknowledges only company work is one that is lacking in harmony of life.

YOUTH: It's exactly as you say! And it's not as if the family he's supporting has any say in the matter, either. You can't argue with your father when he growls with a violent tone of voice, 'It's thanks to me that there's food on the table.'

PHILOSOPHER: Such a father has probably been able to recognise his own worth only on the level of acts. He works all those hours, brings in enough money to support a family, and is recognised by society—and, on that basis, he views himself as having greater worth than the other members of his family. For each and every one of us, however, there comes a time when one can no longer serve as the provider. When one gets older and reaches retirement age, for example, one may have no choice but to live off one's pension or support from one's children. Even when one is young, injury or poor health can lead to not being able work any longer. On such occasions, those who can accept themselves only on the level of acts are severely damaged.

YOUTH: You mean those people whose lifestyle is all about work?

PHILOSOPHER: Yes. People whose lives lack harmony.

YOUTH: In that case, I think I'm starting to get what you mean by the level of being, which you brought up last time. And I certainly haven't given much thought to the fact that someday I won't be able to work any longer, or do anything on the level of acts.

PHILOSOPHER: Does one accept oneself on the level of acts, or on the level of being? This is truly a question that relates to the courage to be happy.

YOU CAN BE HAPPY NOW

YOUTH: The courage to be happy. Well, let's hear what *kind* of courage that should be.

PHILOSOPHER: Yes, that is an important point.

YOUTH: You say that all problems are interpersonal relationship problems. And then you turn that around, and say that our happiness is to be found in our interpersonal relations, too. But I still find these aspects hard to accept. Is what human beings call happiness merely something within our good interpersonal relations? That is to say, do our lives exist for such minuscule repose and joy?

PHILOSOPHER: I have a good idea of the issues you are grappling with. The first time I attended a lecture on Adlerian psychology, the lecturer, Oscar Christensen, who was a disciple of one of Adler's disciples, made the following statement: 'Those who hear my talk today can be happy right now, this very instant. But those who do not will never be able to be happy.'

YOUTH: Wow! That's straight from the mouth of a con man. You're not telling me you fell for that, are you?

PHILOSOPHER: What is happiness to human beings? This is a subject that has been one of the consistent threads of philosophy since ancient times. I had always regarded psychology as nothing more than a field of philosophy, and as such had very little interest in psychology as a whole. So, it was as a student of philosophy that I had concerned myself, in my own way, with the question: what is happiness?' I would be remiss if I did not admit to having felt some reluctance on hearing Christensen's words. However, at the same time that I experienced that reluctance, I realised something. I had given much deep thought to the true character of happiness. I had searched for answers. But I had not always given deep thought to the question: how can one be happy? It occurred to me then that even though I was a student of philosophy, maybe I wasn't happy.

YOUTH: I see. So, your first encounter with Adlerian psychology began with a feeling of incongruity?

PHILOSOPHER: That's right.

YOUTH: Then, please tell me: did you eventually become happy?

PHILOSOPHER: Of course.

YOUTH: How can you be so sure?

PHILOSOPHER: For a human being, the greatest unhappiness is not being able to like oneself. Adler came up with an extremely simple answer to address this reality. Namely, that the feeling of 'I am beneficial to the community' or 'I am of use to someone' is the only thing that can give one a true awareness that one has worth.

YOUTH: Do you mean the 'contribution to others' you mentioned earlier?

PHILOSOPHER: Yes. And this is an important point: when we speak of contribution to others, it doesn't matter if the contribution is not a visible one.

YOUTH: It doesn't matter if the contribution is not a visible one?

PHILOSOPHER: You are not the one who decides if your contributions are of use. That is the task of other people, and is not an issue in which you can intervene. In principle, there is not even any way you can know whether you have really made a contribution. That is to say, when we are engaging in this contribution to others, the contribution does not have to be a visible one—all we need is the subjective sense that 'I am of use to someone', or in other words, a feeling of contribution.

YOUTH: Wait a minute! If that's the case, then what you are calling happiness is . . .

PHILOSOPHER: Do you see it now? In a word, happiness is the feeling of contribution. That is the definition of happiness.

YOUTH: But, but that's . . .

PHILOSOPHER: Is something wrong?

YOUTH: There's no way I can accept such a simplistic definition. Look, I'm not forgetting what you told me before. You said, 'Though on the level of acts, one might not be of use to anyone, on the level of being, every person is of use.' But if that's the case, according to your logic, all human beings would be happy!

PHILOSOPHER: All human beings can be happy. But it must be understood—this does not mean all human beings *are* happy. Whether it is on the level of acts or on the level of being, one needs to *feel* that one is of use to someone. That is to say, one needs a feeling of contribution.

YOUTH: So, you are saying that the reason I am not happy is that I don't have a feeling of contribution?

PHILOSOPHER: That is correct.

YOUTH: Then how can I get a feeling of contribution? By working? Through volunteer activities?

PHILOSOPHER: Earlier, we were talking about desire for recognition. In response to my statement that one must not seek recognition, you said that desire for recognition is a universal desire.

YOUTH: Yes, I did. But honestly, I'm still not entirely certain about this point.

PHILOSOPHER: But I am sure that the reason people seek recognition is clear to you now. People want to like themselves. They want to feel that they have worth. In order to feel that, they want a feeling of contribution that tells them 'I am of use to someone'. And they seek recognition from others as an easy means for gaining that feeling of contribution.

YOUTH: You are saying that desire for recognition is a means for gaining a feeling of contribution?

PHILOSOPHER: Isn't it so?

YOUTH: No way. That contradicts everything you've been saying until now. Because isn't receiving recognition from others supposed to be a means for gaining a feeling of contribution? And then you say, 'Happiness is the feeling of contribution.' If it is, then fulfilling one's desire for recognition is directly linked with happiness, isn't it? Ha-ha! At last, you've acknowledged the necessity of the desire for recognition.

PHILOSOPHER: You are forgetting an important issue. If one's means for gaining a feeling of contribution turns out to be 'being recognised by others', in the long run, one will have no choice but to walk through life in accordance with other people's wishes. There is no freedom in a feeling of contribution that is gained through the desire for recognition. We are beings who choose freedom while aspiring to happiness.

YOUTH: So, one can have happiness only if one has freedom?

PHILOSOPHER: Yes. Freedom as an institution may differ depending on the country, the times or the culture. But freedom in our inter-personal relations is universal.

YOUTH: There's no way that you will acknowledge the desire for recognition?

PHILOSOPHER: If one really has a feeling of contribution, one will no longer have any need for recognition from others. Because one will already have the real awareness that 'I am of use to someone', without needing to go out of one's way to be acknowledged by others. In other words, a person who is obsessed with the desire for recognition does not have any community feeling yet, and has not managed to engage in self-acceptance, confidence in others or contribution to others.

YOUTH: So, if one just has community feeling, the desire for recognition will disappear?

PHILOSOPHER: Yes, it will disappear. There is no need for recognition from others.

The philosopher's points could be summed up as follows: people can only be truly aware of their worth when they are able to feel 'I am of use to someone'. However, it doesn't matter if the contribution one makes at such a time is without any visible form. It is enough to have the subjective sense of being of use to someone, that is to say, a feeling of contribution. And then, the philosopher arrives at the following conclusion: happiness is the feeling of contribution. There certainly seemed to be aspects of the truth there. *But is that really all that happiness is? Not if it's the happiness I'm searching for!*

TWO PATHS TRAVELLED BY THOSE WANTING TO BE 'SPECIAL BEINGS'

YOUTH: You still have not answered my question. Maybe I could actually learn to like myself through contribution to others. Maybe I could come to feel that I have worth, that I am not a worthless being. But is that all a person needs to be happy? Having come into this world, I think that unless I am able to accomplish the sort of grand undertaking that future generations will remember me for, unless I can prove myself as 'I, who am no one else but me,' I will never find true happiness. You are trying to frame everything within interpersonal relations without saying a thing about self-realising happiness. If you ask me, that's nothing but evasion!

PHILOSOPHER: I'm not really sure what you mean by 'self-realising happiness'. What exactly are you referring to?

YOUTH: It's something that is different for each person. I suppose there are those who want to succeed in society, and those who have more personal objectives – a researcher endeavouring to develop a wonder drug, for instance, or an artist who strives to create a satisfying body of work.

PHILOSOPHER: What is it for you?

YOUTH: I still don't really know what I am looking for or what I'll want to do in the future. But I know that I've got to do something. There's no way I'm going to spend the rest of my days working in a university library. When I find a dream that I can devote my life to, and I attain self-realisation, that's when I'll experience true happiness. My father was someone who buried himself in his work from day to night, and I have no idea if that was happiness to him or not. To my eyes, at least, he seemed forever busy and never happy. That is not the kind of life I want to lead.

PHILOSOPHER: All right. If you think about this point using children who engage in problem behaviour as an example, it might be easier to grasp.

YOUTH: Problem behaviour?

PHILOSOPHER: That's right. First of all, we human beings have a universal desire that is referred to as 'pursuit of superiority'. Do you recall our discussion of this?

YOUTH: Yes. Simply put, it's a term that indicates 'hoping to improve' and 'pursuing an ideal state'.

PHILOSOPHER: There are many children who, in their early stages, try to be especially good. In particular, they obey their parents, comport themselves in a socially acceptable manner, and apply themselves assiduously to their studies and in sports, and excel in extracurricular activities as well. In this way, they try to get their parents to acknowledge them. However, when being especially good does not work out—their studies or sports don't go well, for example—they do an about-face and try to be especially bad.

YOUTH: Why do they do that?

PHILOSOPHER: Whether they are trying to be especially good, or trying to be especially bad, the goal is the same: to attract the attention of other people, get out of the 'normal' condition and become a 'special being'. That is their only goal.

YOUTH: Hmm. All right, please go on.

PHILOSOPHER: In any case, whether it is one's studies or one's participation in sports, either way one needs to make a constant effort if one is to produce any kind of significant results. But the children who try to be especially bad—that is to say, the ones who engage in problem behaviour—are endeavouring to attract the attention of other people even as they continue to avoid any such healthy effort. In Adlerian psychology, this is referred to as the 'pursuit of easy superiority'. Take, for example, the problem child who disrupts lessons by throwing erasers or speaking in a loud voice. He is certain to get the attention of his friends and teachers. Even if it is something that is limited to that place, he will probably succeed in becoming a special being. But that is a pursuit of easy superiority, and is an unhealthy attitude.

YOUTH: So, children who commit delinquent acts are engaging in the pursuit of easy superiority, too?

PHILOSOPHER: Yes, they are. All types of problem behaviour, from refusing to attend school, to wrist-cutting, to underage drinking and smoking and so on, are forms of the pursuit of easy superiority. And your shut-in friend, who you told me about at the beginning, is engaging in it, too. When a child engages in problem behaviour, his parents and other adults rebuke him. Being rebuked, more than anything else, puts stress on the child. But even if it is in the form of rebuke, the child wants his parents' attention. He wants to be a special being, and the form that attention takes doesn't matter. So, in a sense, it is only natural that he does not stop engaging in problem behaviour, no matter how harshly he is rebuked.

YOUTH: It's because of their rebuking that he doesn't stop the problem behaviour?

PHILOSOPHER: Exactly. Because the parents and other adults are giving him attention through the act of rebuking.

YOUTH: But previously, you spoke of the goal of problem behaviour as being revenge on the parents, right? Does that connect with this in some way?

PHILOSOPHER: Yes. 'Revenge' and 'pursuit of easy superiority' are easily linked. One makes trouble for another person, while trying at the same time to be 'special'.

THE COURAGE TO BE NORMAL

YOUTH: But how . . . ? It would be impossible for all human beings to be especially good, or anything like that, wouldn't it? No matter what, people have their strengths and weaknesses, and there will always be differences. There's only a handful of geniuses in the world, and not everyone is cut out to be an honours student. So, for all the losers, there's nothing for it besides being especially bad.

PHILOSOPHER: Yes, it's that Socratic paradox, that no one desires evil. Because to children who engage in problem behaviour, even violent acts and theft are accomplishments of 'good'.

YOUTH: But that's horrible! That's a line of reasoning with no way out.

PHILOSOPHER: What Adlerian psychology emphasises at this juncture are the words 'the courage to be normal'.

YOUTH: The courage to be normal?

PHILOSOPHER: Why is it necessary to be special? Probably because one cannot accept one's normal self. And it is precisely for this reason that when being especially good becomes a lost cause, one makes the huge leap to being specially bad—the opposite extreme. But is being normal, being ordinary, really such a bad thing? Is it something inferior? Or, in truth, isn't everybody normal? It is necessary to think this through to its logical conclusion.

YOUTH: So, are you saying that I should be normal?

PHILOSOPHER: Self-acceptance is the vital first step. If you are able to possess the courage to be normal, your way of looking at the world will change dramatically.

YOUTH: But . . .

PHILOSOPHER: You are probably rejecting normality because you equate being normal with being incapable. Being normal is not being incapable. One does not need to flaunt one's superiority.

YOUTH: Fine, I acknowledge the danger of aiming to be special. But does one really need to make the deliberate choice to be normal? If I pass my time in this world in an utterly humdrum way, if I lead a pointless life without leaving any record or memory of my existence whatsoever, am I to just be satisfied with my lot, because that's the sort of human being I am? You've got to be joking. I'd abandon such a life in a second!

PHILOSOPHER: You want to be special, no matter what?

YOUTH: No! Look, accepting what you call 'normal' would lead to me having to affirm my idle self! It would just be saying, 'This is all I am capable of and that's fine.' I refuse to accept such an idle way of life. Do you think that Napoleon or Alexander the Great, or Einstein or Martin Luther King accepted 'normal'? And how about Socrates and Plato? Not a chance! More than likely, they all lived their lives while carrying the torch of a great ideal or objective. Another Napoleon could never emerge with your line of reasoning. You are trying to rid the world of geniuses!

PHILOSOPHER: So, what you are saying is that one needs lofty goals in life.

YOUTH: But that's obvious!

'The courage to be normal'—what truly dreadful words. Are Adler and this philosopher really telling me to choose such a path? To go about my life as just another soul among the utterly ordinary, faceless masses? I'm no genius, of course. Maybe 'normal' is the only choice I have. Maybe I will just have to accept my mediocre self and surrender to leading a mediocre, everyday existence. But I will fight it. Whatever happens, I will oppose this man to the bitter end. We seem to be approaching the heart of our discussion. **The young man's pulse was racing, and despite the wintry chill in the air, his clenched fists shone with sweat.**

LIFE IS A SERIES OF MOMENTS

PHILOSOPHER: All right. When you speak of lofty goals, I am guessing that you have an image of something like a mountain climber aiming for the top.

YOUTH: Yes, that's right. People, myself included, aim for the top of the mountain.

PHILOSOPHER: But, if life were climbing a mountain in order to reach the top, then the greater part of life would end up being 'en route'. That is to say, one's 'real life' would begin with one's trek on the mountainside, and the distance one has travelled up until that point would be a 'tentative life' led by a 'tentative me'.

YOUTH: I guess that's one way of putting it. The way I am now, I am definitely an 'en-route' person.

PHILOSOPHER: Now, supposing you didn't make it to the mountaintop, what would that mean for your life? With accidents and diseases and the like, people don't always make it all the way, and mountain climbing itself is fraught with pitfalls and often ends in failure. So, one's life would be interrupted 'en route', with just this 'tentative me' leading a 'tentative life'. What kind of life would that be?

YOUTH: That's . . . Well, that'd be a case of getting one's just desserts. So, I didn't have the ability, or I didn't have the physical strength to climb a mountain, or I wasn't lucky, or I lacked the skill—that's all! Yes, that is a reality I am prepared to accept.

PHILOSOPHER: Adlerian psychology has a different standpoint. People who think of life as being like climbing a mountain are treating their own existences as lines. As if there is a line that started the instant one came into this world, and that continues in all manner of curves of varying sizes until it arrives at the summit, and then at long last reaches its terminus, which is death. This conception, which treats life as a kind of story, is an idea that links with Freudian aetiology (the attributing of causes), and is a way of thinking that makes the greater part of life into something that is 'en route'.

YOUTH: Well, what is your image of life?

PHILOSOPHER: Do not treat it as a line. Think of life as a series of dots. If you look through a magnifying glass at a solid line drawn with chalk, you will discover that what you thought was a line is actually a series of small dots. Seemingly linear existence is actually a series of dots; in other words, life is a series of moments.

YOUTH: A series of moments?

PHILOSOPHER: Yes. It is a series of moments called 'now'. We can live only in the here and now. Our lives exist only in moments. Adults who do not know this attempt to impose 'linear' lives onto young people. Their thinking is that staying on the conventional tracks—good university, big company, stable household—is a happy life. But life is not made up of lines or anything like that.

YOUTH: So, there's no need for life planning or career planning?

PHILOSOPHER: If life were a line, then life planning would be possible. But our lives are only a series of dots. A well-planned life is not something to be treated as necessary or unnecessary, as it is impossible.

YOUTH: Oh, nonsense! What an absurd idea!

LIVE LIKE YOU'RE DANCING

PHILOSOPHER: What is wrong with it?

YOUTH: Your argument not only denies the making of plans in life, it goes as far as to deny even making efforts. Take, for example, the life of someone who has dreamed of being a violinist ever since childhood, and who, after years of strict training, has at long last become an active member in a celebrated orchestra. Or another life, one of intensive studies that successfully leads to the passing of the bar examination and to becoming a lawyer. Neither of these lives would be possible without objectives and plans.

PHILOSOPHER: So, in other words, like mountain climbers aiming to reach the mountaintop, they have persevered on their paths?

YOUTH: Of course!

PHILOSOPHER: But is that really the case? Isn't it that these people have lived each and every instant of their lives here and now? That is to say, rather than living lives that are 'en route', they are always living here and now. For example, the person who had dreams of becoming a violinist was always looking at pieces of music, and concentrating on each piece, and on each and every measure and note.

YOUTH: Would they attain their objectives that way?

PHILOSOPHER: Think of it this way: Life is a series of moments, which one lives as if one were dancing, right now, around and around each passing instant. And when one happens to survey one's surroundings, one realises, *I guess I've made it this far*. Among those who have danced the dance of the violin, there are people who stay the course and become professional musicians. Among those who have danced the dance of the bar examination, there are people who become lawyers. There are people who have danced the dance of writing, and become authors. Of course, it also happens that people end up in entirely different places. But none of these lives came to an end 'en route'. It is enough if one finds fulfilment in the here and now one is dancing.

YOUTH: It's enough if one can dance in the now?

PHILOSOPHER: Yes. With dance, it is the dancing itself that is the goal, and no one is concerned with arriving somewhere by doing it. Naturally, it may happen that one arrives somewhere as a result of having danced. Since one is dancing, one does not stay in the same place. But there is no destination.

YOUTH: A life without a destination, who ever heard of such a thing? Who would acknowledge such an unsteady life, that bends whichever way the wind blows?

PHILOSOPHER: The kind of life that you speak of, which tries to reach a destination, may be termed a 'kinetic (dynamic) life'. By contrast, the kind of dancing life I am talking about could be called an 'energeial (actual-active-state) life'.

YOUTH: Kinetic? Energeial?

PHILOSOPHER: Let's refer to Aristotle's explanation. Ordinary motion—which is referred to as *kinesis*—has a starting point and an end point. The movement from the starting point to the end point is optimal if it is carried out as efficiently and as quickly as possible. If one can take an express train, there is no need to ride the local one that makes every stop.

YOUTH: In other words, if one's destination is to become a lawyer, it's best to get there as quickly and as efficiently as one can.

PHILOSOPHER: Yes. And the road one takes to get to that destination is, in the sense that one's goal has not yet been reached, incomplete. This is kinetic life.

YOUTH: Because it's halfway?

PHILOSOPHER: That's right. *Energeia*, on the other hand, is a kind of movement in which what is 'now forming' is what 'has been formed'.

YOUTH: What is 'now forming' is what 'has been formed'?

PHILOSOPHER: One might also think of it as movement in which the process itself is treated as the outcome. Dance is like that, and so is a journey.

YOUTH: Ah, I'm getting confused . . . What is this about a journey?

PHILOSOPHER: What kind of goal is the act of going on a journey? Suppose you are going on a journey to Egypt. Would you try to arrive at the Great Pyramid of Giza as efficiently and quickly as possible, and then head straight back home by the shortest route? One would not call that a 'journey'. You should be on a journey the moment you step outside your home, and all the moments on the way to your destination should be a journey. Of course, there might be circumstances that prevent you from making it to the pyramid, but that does not mean you didn't go on a journey. This is 'energeial life'.

YOUTH: I guess I'm just not getting this. Weren't you refuting the kind of value system of aiming for the mountaintop? What happens if you liken energeial life to mountain climbing?

PHILOSOPHER: If the goal of climbing a mountain were to get to the top, that would be a kinetic act. To take it to the extreme, it wouldn't matter if you went to the mountaintop in a helicopter, stayed there for five minutes or so, and then headed back in the helicopter again. Of course, if you didn't make it to the mountaintop, that would mean the mountain-climbing expedition was a failure. However, if the goal is mountain climbing itself, and not just getting to the top, one could say it is energeial. In this case, in the end it doesn't matter whether one makes it to the mountaintop or not.

YOUTH: That sort of argument is just ridiculous! You've fallen into a completely self-defeating contradiction. Before you lose face before the whole wide world, I'll cut through your shameless nonsense, once and for all.

PHILOSOPHER: Oh, I'd be much obliged.

SHINE A LIGHT ON THE
HERE AND NOW

YOUTH: Look, in your refutation of aetiology, you rejected focusing on the past. You said that the past does not exist, and that it has no meaning. I acknowledge those points. It is true that one cannot change the past. If there is something that can be changed, it is the future. But now, by advocating this energeia way of living, you are refuting planning; that is to say, you are rejecting even changing one's future of one's own volition. So, while you reject looking back, you are rejecting looking forward, too. It's like you're telling me to just walk blindfolded along a pathless path.

PHILOSOPHER: You can see neither behind you, nor in front of you?

YOUTH: That's right, I can't see!

PHILOSOPHER: Isn't that only natural? Where is the problem here?

YOUTH: What? What are you talking about?

PHILOSOPHER: Imagine that you are standing on a theatre stage. If the house lights are on, you'll probably be able to see all the way to the back of the hall. But if you're under a bright spotlight, you won't be able to make out even the front row. That's exactly how it is with our lives. It's because we cast a dim light on our entire lives that we are able to see the past and the future. Or, at least we imagine we can. But if one is shining a bright spotlight on here and now, one cannot see the past or the future anymore.

YOUTH: A bright spotlight?

PHILOSOPHER: Yes. We should live more earnestly only here and now. The fact that you think you can see the past, or predict the future, is proof that rather than living earnestly here and now, you are living in a dim twilight. Life is a series of moments, and neither the past nor the future exist. You are trying to give yourself a way out by focusing on the past and the future. What happened in the past has nothing whatsoever to do with your here and now, and what the future may hold is not a matter to think about here and now. If you are living earnestly here and now, you will not be concerned with such things.

YOUTH: But . . .

PHILOSOPHER: When one adopts the point of view of Freudian aetiology, one sees life as a kind of great big story based on cause and effect. So, then, it's all about where and when I was born, what my childhood was like, the school I attended and the company where I got a job. And that decides who I am now, and who I will become. To be sure, likening one's life to a story is probably an entertaining job. The problem is, one can see the dimness that lies ahead at the end of the story. Moreover, one will try to lead a life that is in line with that story. And then one says, my life is such-and-such, so I have no choice but to live this way, and it's not because of me—it's my past, it's the environment, and so on. But bringing up the past here is nothing but a way out, a life-lie. However, life is a series of dots, a series of moments. If you can grasp that you will not need a story any longer.

YOUTH: If you put it that way, the lifestyle that Adler is advocating is a kind of story, too.

PHILOSOPHER: Lifestyle is about here and now, and is something that one can change of one's own volition. The life of the past that looks like a straight line only appears that way to you as a result of your making ceaseless resolutions to not change. The life that lies ahead of you is a completely blank page, and there are no tracks that have been laid for you to follow. There is no story there.

YOUTH: But that's just living for the moment. Or worse, a vicious hedonism!

PHILOSOPHER: No. To shine a spotlight on here and now is to go about doing what one can do now, earnestly and conscientiously.

THE GREATEST LIFE-LIE

YOUTH: To live earnestly and conscientiously?

PHILOSOPHER: For example, one wants to get into a university, but one makes no attempt to study. This an attitude of not living earnestly here and now. Of course, maybe the entrance examination is still far off. Maybe one is not sure what needs to be studied or how thoroughly, and one finds it troublesome. However, it is enough to do it little by little—every day one can work out some mathematical formulas; one can memorise some words. In short, one can dance the dance. By doing so, one is sure to have a sense of 'this is what I did today'; this is what today, this single day, was for. Clearly, today is not for an entrance examination in the distant future. And the same thing would hold true for your father, too—he was likely dancing earnestly the dance of his everyday work. He lived earnestly here and now, without having a grand objective or the need to achieve that objective. And, if that was the case, it would seem that your father's life was a happy one.

YOUTH: Are you telling me to affirm that way of living? That I should accept my father's constantly work-burdened existence . . . ?

PHILOSOPHER: There is no need to make yourself affirm it. Only, instead of seeing his life as a line that he reached, start seeing how he lived it, see the moments of his life.

YOUTH: The moments.

PHILOSOPHER: And the same may be said with regard to your own life. You set objectives for the distant future, and think of now as your preparatory period. You think, *I really want to do this, and I'll do it when the time comes.* This is a way of living that postpones life. As long as we postpone life, we can never go anywhere, and will only pass our days one after the next in dull monotony, because we think of here and now as just a preparatory period, as a time for patience. But a 'here and now' in which one is studying for an entrance examination in the distant future, for example, is the real thing.

YOUTH: Okay, I'll accept that. I can certainly accept living earnestly here and now, and not setting up some fabricated line. But, I don't have any dreams or objectives in my life. I don't know what dance to do. My here and now is nothing but utterly useless moments.

PHILOSOPHER: Not having objectives or the like is fine. Living earnestly here and now is itself a dance. One must not get too serious. Please do not confuse being earnest with being too serious.

YOUTH: Be earnest, but not too serious.

PHILOSOPHER: That's right. Life is always simple, not something that one needs to get too serious about. If one is living each moment earnestly, there is no need to get too serious.

And there is another thing I would like you to keep in mind. When one has adopted an energeial viewpoint, life is always complete.

YOUTH: It's complete?

PHILOSOPHER: If your life, or mine for that matter, were to come to an end here and now, it would not do to refer to either of them as unhappy. The life that ends at the age of twenty and the life that ends at ninety are both complete lives, and lives of happiness.

YOUTH: So, if I have lived earnestly here and now, those moments will always be complete?

PHILOSOPHER: Exactly. Now, I have used the word 'life-lie' again and again throughout our discussion. I would like to conclude by talking about the greatest life-lie of all.

YOUTH: Please do.

PHILOSOPHER: The greatest life-lie of all is to not live here and now. It is to look at the past and the future, cast a dim light on one's entire life, and believe that one has been able to see something. Until now, you have turned away from the here and now, and only shone a light on invented pasts and futures. You have told a great lie to your life, to these irreplaceable moments.

YOUTH: Oh, okay!

PHILOSOPHER: So, cast away the life-lie, and fearlessly shine a bright spotlight on here and now. That is something you can do.

YOUTH: That is something I can do? Do you think I have in me the *courage* to live out these moments earnestly, without resorting to the life-lie?

PHILOSOPHER: Since neither the past nor the future exist, let's talk about now. It's not yesterday or tomorrow that decides it. It's here and now.

GIVE MEANING TO SEEMINGLY
MEANINGLESS LIFE

YOUTH: What are you saying?

PHILOSOPHER: I think this discussion has now reached the water's edge. Whether you drink the water or not is entirely up to you.

YOUTH: Ah, maybe Adlerian psychology, and your philosophy, are actually changing me. Maybe I am trying to let go of my resolve not to change, and choose a new way of living, a new lifestyle . . . But wait, there is one last thing I'd like to ask.

PHILOSOPHER: And what would that be?

YOUTH: When life is taken as a series of moments, as existing only here and now, what meaning could it possibly have? For what was I born, and for what am I enduring this life of hardship until I reach my last gasp? The point of it all is beyond me.

PHILOSOPHER: What is the meaning of life? What are people living for? When someone posed these questions to Adler, this was his answer: 'Life in general has no meaning.'

YOUTH: Life is meaningless?

PHILOSOPHER: The world in which we live is constantly beset by all manner of horrendous events, and we exist with the ravages of war and natural disasters all around us. When confronted by the fact of children dying in the turmoil of war, there is no way one can go on about the meaning of life. In other words, there is no meaning in using generalisations to talk about life. But being confronted by such incomprehensible tragedies without taking any action is tantamount to affirming them. Regardless of the circumstances, we must take some form of action. We must stand up to Kant's 'inclination'.

YOUTH: Yes!

PHILOSOPHER: Now, suppose one experiences a major natural disaster, and one's response is to look back at the past in an aetiological manner and say, 'What could have caused such a thing to happen?' How meaningful would that be? An experience of hardship should be an opportunity to look ahead and think, *What can I do from now on?*

YOUTH: I agree entirely!

PHILOSOPHER: And Adler, having stated that 'life in general has no meaning', then continues, 'Whatever meaning life has must be assigned to it by the individual.'

YOUTH: Assigned to it by the individual? What does that mean?

PHILOSOPHER: During the war, my grandfather was firebombed, and his face was severely burned. In every way, it was a horrendous and inhumane event. It would certainly have been within the realm of possibility for him to choose a lifestyle with the perspective of 'the world is a horrible place', or 'people are my enemies'. However, when my grandfather rode the train on visits to the hospital, there were always other passengers who would give up their seats for him. This is something I heard about through my mother, so I do not know how he actually felt. But this is what I believe: my grandfather chose a lifestyle with the perspective of 'people are my comrades, and the world is a wonderful place'. That is exactly what Adler is pointing to when he says whatever meaning life has must be assigned to it by the individual. So, life in general has no meaning whatsoever. But you can assign meaning to that life. And you are the only one who can assign meaning to your life.

YOUTH: Then, please tell me! How can I assign proper meaning to a meaningless life? I do not have the confidence yet!

PHILOSOPHER: You are lost in your life. Why are you lost? You are lost because you are trying to choose freedom; that is to say, a path on which you are not afraid of being disliked by others and you are not living others' lives—a path that is yours alone.

YOUTH: That's right! I want to choose happiness, and choose freedom!

PHILOSOPHER: When one attempts to choose freedom, it is only natural that one may lose one's way. At this juncture, Adlerian psychology holds up a 'guiding star' as a grand compass pointing to a life of freedom.

YOUTH: A guiding star?

PHILOSOPHER: Just like the traveller who relies on the North Star, in our lives we need a guiding star. That is the Adlerian psychology way of thinking. It is an expansive ideal that says, as long as we do not lose sight of this compass and keep on moving in this direction, there is happiness.

YOUTH: Where is that star?

PHILOSOPHER: It is contribution to others.

YOUTH: Huh? Contribution to others!

PHILOSOPHER: No matter what moments you are living, or if there are people who dislike you, as long as you do not lose sight of the guiding star of 'I contribute to others', you will not lose your way, and you can do whatever you like. Whether you're disliked or not, you pay it no mind and live free.

YOUTH: If I have the star of contribution to others high in the sky above me, I will always have happiness and comrades by my side.

PHILOSOPHER: Then, let's dance in earnest the moments of the here and now, and live in earnest. Do not look at the past, and do not look at the future. One lives each complete moment like a dance. There is no need to compete with anyone, and one has no use for destinations. As long as you are dancing, you will get somewhere.

YOUTH: A 'somewhere' that no one else knows!

PHILOSOPHER: That is the nature of energeial life. If I look back on my own life up to now, no matter how I try, I will never arrive at a satisfactory explanation as to why I am here and now. Though, at one time, the study of Greek philosophy was my focus, before long I took up the study of Adlerian psychology in tandem with it, and here I am today, deep in conversation with you, my irreplaceable friend. It is the result of having danced the moments—that is the only way to explain it. When you have danced here and now in earnest and to the full, that is when the meaning of your life will become clear to you.

YOUTH: It will? I . . . I believe you!

PHILOSOPHER: Yes, please believe. Through my many years living with Adler's thought, there is something I have noticed.

YOUTH: And that is?

PHILOSOPHER: It is that the power of one person is great, or, rather, 'my power is immeasurably great'.

YOUTH: What do you mean?

PHILOSOPHER: Well, in other words, if 'I' change, the world will change. This means that the world can be changed only by me and no one else will change it for me. The world that has appeared to me since learning of Adlerian psychology is not the world I once knew.

YOUTH: If I change, the world will change. No one else will change the world for me . . .

PHILOSOPHER: It is similar to the shock experienced by someone who, after many years of being nearsighted, puts on glasses for the first time. Previously indistinct outlines of the world become well defined, and even the colours are more vivid. Furthermore, it is not only a part of one's visual field that becomes clear, but the entire visible world. I can only imagine how happy you will be if you have a similar experience.

YOUTH: Ah, if only I'd known! I wish I had known this ten years ago, or even just five years ago. If only I had known five years ago, before I got a job . . .

PHILOSOPHER: No, that is not the case. You say you wish you had known this ten years ago. It is because Adler's thought resonates with you now that you are thinking this. No one knows how you would have felt about it ten years ago. This discussion was something that you needed to hear now.

YOUTH: Yes, I certainly did!

PHILOSOPHER: One more time, I give you the words of Adler: 'Someone has to start. Other people might not be cooperative, but that is not connected to you. My advice is this: You should start. With no regard to whether others are cooperative or not.'

YOUTH: I cannot tell yet if it is I who have changed, or if it is the world that I can see from that vantage point that has changed. But there is one thing I can say with conviction: here and now is shining brightly! Yes, it is so bright that I can see almost nothing of tomorrow.

PHILOSOPHER: I believe that you have drunk the water. So, young friend who walks ahead, shall we walk together?

YOUTH: I believe you, too. Yes, let's walk together. And thank you for all your time.

PHILOSOPHER: Thank you, too.

YOUTH: I hope you will not mind if, at some point, I visit you here again. Yes, as an irreplaceable friend. And I won't be saying anything more about taking apart your arguments.

PHILOSOPHER: Ha-ha! At last, you have shown me a young person's smile. Well, it's quite late already. Let's pass our own nights, and greet the new morning.

The young man slowly tied his shoelaces and left the philosopher's house. On opening the door, a snowy scene spread out before him. The full moon, its floating form obscured, illuminated the shimmering whiteness at his feet. *What clear air. What dazzling light. I am going to tread on this fresh snow, and take my first step.* **The young man drew a deep breath, rubbed the slight stubble on his face, and murmured emphatically, 'The world is simple, and life is too.'**

AFTERWORD

In life, there are encounters in which a book one happens to pick up one day ends up completely altering one's landscape the following morning.

It was the winter of 1999, and I was a youth in my twenties, when I had the great fortune of encountering such a book at a bookshop in Ikebukuro. This was Ichiro Kishimi's *Adorā Shinrigaku Nyūmon* (*Introduction to Adlerian Psychology*).

Here was a form of thought, profound in every way, yet conveyed in simple language, that seemed to overturn our accepted wisdoms at their very roots. A Copernican revolution that denied trauma and converted aetiology into teleology. Having always felt something unconvincing in the discourses of the Freudians and Jungians, I was affected very deeply. Who was this Alfred Adler? How had I never known of his existence before? I purchased every single book by or about Adler that I could get my hands on, and became completely engrossed and read them over and over again.

But I was struck then by a certain fact. What I was interested in was not solely Adlerian psychology, but rather something that had emerged through the filter of the philosopher, Ichiro Kishimi: it was Kishimi–Adler studies that I was seeking.

Grounded in the thought of Socrates and Plato and other ancient Greek philosophers, the Adlerian psychology that Kishimi conveys to us reveals Adler as a thinker, a philosopher, whose work went far beyond the confines of clinical psychology. For instance, the statement 'It is only in social contexts that a person becomes an individual' is positively Hegelian; in his laying emphasis on subjective interpretation over objective truth, he echoes Nietzsche's worldview; and ideas recalling the phenomenology of Husserl and Heidegger are in abundance.

Adlerian psychology, which draws inspiration from these philosophical insights to proclaim 'all problems are interpersonal relationship problems', 'people can change and be happy from this moment onward' and 'the problem is not one of ability, but of courage' was to utterly change the worldview of this rather confused youth.

Nevertheless, there was almost no one around me who had heard of Adlerian psychology. Eventually, it occurred to me that I would like to make a book some day with Kishimi that would be a definitive edition of Adlerian psychology (Kishimi–Adler studies), and I contacted one editor after another and waited impatiently for the opportunity to arise.

It was in March 2010 that I was at last able to meet with Kishimi, who lives in Kyoto. More than ten years had passed since my first reading of *Introduction to Adlerian Psychology*.

When Kishimi said to me then, 'Socrates' thought was conveyed by Plato. I would like to be a Plato for Adler,' without a second thought, I answered, 'Then, I will be a Plato for you, Mr Kishimi.' And that is how this book was conceived.

One aspect of Adler's simple and universal ideas is that there are times when he may seem to be stating the obvious, while at others he is likely to be regarded as espousing utterly unrealisable, idealistic theories.

Accordingly, in this book, in hopes of focusing on any doubts that might be harboured by the reader, I have adopted the format of a dialogue between a philosopher and a young man.

As is implied in this narrative, it is not a simple thing to make the ideas of Adler one's own and put them into practice. There are points that make one want to rebel, statements that are difficult to accept, and proposals that one may struggle to grasp.

But the ideas of Adler have the power to completely change a person's life, just like they did for me over a decade ago. Then, it is only a question of having the courage to take a step forward.

In closing, I would like to express my deep gratitude to Ichiro Kishimi, who never treated me as a disciple, even though I was much younger than he, but met me forthrightly as a friend; to the editor Yoshifumi Kakiuchi, for his steadfast and unstinting support at every step of the way; and last but not least, to all the readers of this book.

Thank you very much.

Fumitake Koga

* * *

More than half a century has passed since the death of Adler, and the times still cannot catch up with the freshness of his ideas. Though compared to Freud or Jung, the name Adler is little known in Japan today. Adler's teachings are said to be a 'communal quarry' that anyone can excavate something from. And though his name often goes unmentioned, the influence of his teachings has spread far and wide.

I had been studying philosophy ever since my late teens, and it was around the time my child was born, when I was in my early thirties, that I first encountered Adlerian psychology. Eudaimonic theory, which investigates the question 'what is happiness?', is one of the central themes of Western philosophy. I had spent many years pondering this question, when I attended the lecture where I first learned of Adlerian psychology. On hearing the lecturer declare from his podium, 'Those who have listened to my talk today will be able to change and be happy from this moment onward,' I felt repulsed. But at the same time, it dawned on me that I had never thought deeply about how I myself can find happiness, and with the notion that 'finding happiness' itself was perhaps easier than I'd imagined, I took an interest in Adlerian psychology.

In this way, I came to study Adlerian psychology side by side with philosophy. I soon realised, however, that I could not study them separately, as two distinct fields.

For instance, the idea of teleology, far from being something that appeared suddenly in Adler's time, is present in the philosophy of Plato and Aristotle. It became clear to me that Adlerian psychology was a way of thinking that lay in the same vein as Greek philosophy. Moreover, I noticed that the dialogues that Socrates engaged in with youths, which Plato recording in writing for posterity, could be said to correspond very closely to the counselling practised today.

Though many people think of philosophy as something difficult to understand, Plato's dialogues do not contain any specialised language.

It is strange that philosophy should be something that is discussed using words understood only by specialists. Because in its original meaning, philosophy refers not to 'wisdom' itself, but to 'love of wisdom', and it is the very process of learning what one does not know and arriving at wisdom that is important.

Whether or not one attains wisdom in the end is not an issue.

A person reading Plato's dialogues today may be surprised to find that the dialogue concerning courage, for instance, ends without arriving at any conclusion.

The youths engaged in dialogues with Socrates never agree with what he says at the outset. They refute his statements thoroughly. This book is continuing in the tradition of philosophy since Socrates, and that is why it follows the format of a dialogue between a philosopher and a youth.

Upon learning of Adlerian psychology, which is another philosophy, I became dissatisfied with the way of living of the researcher who only reads and interprets the writings of his predecessors. I wanted to engage in dialogues in the way that Socrates did, and eventually I began to practise counselling at psychiatry clinics and other venues.

In doing so, I met many youths.

All of these youths wanted to live sincerely, but many of them were people who had been told by worldly, jaded elders to 'be more realistic', and were on the verge of giving up on their dreams; people who had been through arduous experiences of being entangled in interpersonal relationships that were complicated precisely because they were pure.

Wanting to live sincerely is an important thing, but it is not enough on its own. Adler tells us that all problems are interpersonal relationship problems. But if one does not know how to build good interpersonal relationships, one may end up trying to satisfy other people's expectations. And, unable to communicate out of fear of hurting other people even when one has something to assert, one may end up abandoning what one really wants to do.

While people may certainly be popular among those they know, and not many people will dislike them perhaps, they will end up being incapable of living their own lives.

To a young person like the youth in this book, who has many problems and has already had a harsh awakening to reality, the views put forward by this philosopher, that this world is a simple place and that anyone can be happy from this day onward, may come as a surprise.

'My psychology is for all people,' says Adler, and dispensing with specialised language much as Plato did, he shows us specific steps for improving our interpersonal relationships.

If Adler's way of thinking is hard to accept, it is because it is a compilation of antitheses to normal social thinking, and because to understand it one must put it into practice in everyday life. Though his words are not difficult, there may be a sense of difficulty like that of imagining the blazing heat of summer in the dead of winter; but I hope that the reader will be able to grasp keys here to solving their interpersonal relationship problems.

The day Fumitake Koga, my collaborator and writer for this book, first visited my study, he said, 'I will be a Plato for you, Mr Kishimi.'

Today the reason we can learn about the philosophy of Socrates, who left no known writings, is that Plato took down his dialogues in written form. But Plato did not simply record what Socrates said. It is thanks to Plato's correct understanding of his words that Socrates' teachings are still conveyed today.

It is thanks to the exceptional powers of understanding of Koga, who persisted in carrying out repeated dialogues with me over a period of several years, that this book has seen the light of day. Both Koga and I often made visits to our teachers in our university days, and the youth in this book could be either one of us, but more than anyone, he is you, who picked up this book. It is my sincere hope that while your doubts may linger, I will be able to support your resolution in all manner of life situations through this dialogue with a philosopher.

Ichiro Kishimi